# *THEATRE ADMINISTRATION*

# THEATRE
# ADMINISTRATION

## ELIZABETH SWEETING

( 1969 )

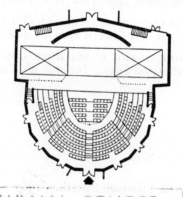

*London*
Sir Isaac Pitman and Sons Ltd

*First Published 1969*

SIR ISAAC PITMAN AND SONS LTD.
Pitman House, Parker Street, Kingsway, London, W.C.2
P.O. Box 6038, Portal Street, Nairobi, Kenya

SIR ISAAC PITMAN (AUST.) PTY. LTD.
Pitman House, Bouverie Street, Carlton, Victoria 3053, Australia

PITMAN PUBLISHING COMPANY S.A. LTD.
P.O. Box 9898, Johannesburg, S. Africa

PITMAN PUBLISHING CORPORATION
6 East 43rd Street, New York, N.Y. 10017, U.S.A.

SIR ISAAC PITMAN (CANADA) LTD.
Pitman House, 381–383 Church Street, Toronto, 3, Canada

THE COPP CLARK PUBLISHING COMPANY
517 Wellington Street, Toronto, 2B, Canada

MADE IN GREAT BRITAIN AT THE PITMAN PRESS, BATH
F9—(G.3502)

# FOREWORD

WHETHER a theatre be large or small, professional or amateur, orthodox or experimental, frivolous or solemnly dedicated, whether it has its own company of players or presents a wide variety of entertainment, whether it is heavily subsidized or is expected to make a profit for shareholders, it must be run as a business. It is a business that exists to sell entertainment to the particular types of customers for which it is catering. Although it is now generally recognized that the theatre and the arts generally justify subsidy from public funds, both national and local, the subsidies can be justified only if there is efficient management and a strict elimination of extravagance and waste. The running costs and overheads must bear a reasonable relationship to box-office receipts. The specialized marketing techniques appropriate to theatre must be applied intelligently and vigorously to the whole area from which the customers can be attracted. Failure to obtain satisfactory audiences does not necessarily imply that the populace has too high a proportion of morons who cannot appreciate the value of the pearls cast before them. It *could* mean that the pearls are spurious. It is unwise to underestimate the intelligence or discrimination of audiences or to minimize the need for expert management.

The theatre manager has a specialized and difficult job. It is not one for the inexperienced enthusiast tempted by the glamour of "show business" or perhaps inspired with a laudable dedication to "culture." Enthusiasm and inspiration are, of course, excellent additions, but realistic competence and a sound commercial instinct are vital necessities. The competence must include a thorough knowledge of how the many varied labours of artists, craftsmen and other workers are fused together to provide what we call good theatre.

The opportunities for the efficient training of potential theatre managers are limited and too little has been written on the subject. The success of the new theatres that have been built in recent years, or that are being planned for the near future, must depend on good management as much as on the provision of good theatrical entertainment, or whatever less realistic word the devotees prefer to use in lieu of "entertainment."

Elizabeth Sweeting speaks with the authority of long experience of doing the job very successfully. She is the Administrator of the Oxford Playhouse—a University Theatre—a member of the Theatre Managers' Association, and of the Executive Committee of the Association of British Theatre Technicians, and is at present on the Arts Council Drama Panel and External Examiner in Drama for the Birmingham Institute of Education. Her book will be welcomed not only by those who hope to become theatre managers: it will become an essential book of reference in every manager's office. And it should be studied by anybody who is involved in the infuriatingly fascinating work of the theatre—professional or amateur. Those who strut and fret their hour upon the stage as well as those who sit and watch them doing it, usually have little knowledge or appreciation of the expertise needed by the host of workers who make the fretting and strutting possible.

PERCY CORRY

# PREFACE

THIS is not intended to be a blue-print of management techniques applicable to each and every theatre, nor could any text-book, I believe, cover all variations and eventualities of the theatre world for those who are courageous enough to want to set up an organization of this kind. It may be of use particularly to those who are planning new theatres of a modest scale in which they intend to include many kinds of activity—professional and amateur theatre and related arts. If it helps anyone, professional or amateur, to avoid some of the traps into which I and others still so often fall even after years of varied experience, it will have served its modest purpose.

A theatre manager is accustomed, as are all who deal with the public in the course of their work, to being asked a multitude of questions on the widest range of subjects. He will readily dispense information about the area in which the theatre is situated, its restaurants, its public transport and its other amenities; about the play showing at the time and about the plays past and to come; about the actors; about the price of seats; about the best places for seeing and hearing (or the worst). But the question at which he will look blank is "What exactly do you do?" The answer can be very brief indeed, to the effect that he does most things and rarely the same things two days running. Or it may be very elaborate and definite. For all those who aspire to become theatre managers this book is meant to guide them through the maze.

Management is not so much a mystique as an attitude of mind, backed by a considerable amount of real knowledge and acquired technique in most branches of the theatre. These are assimilated by personal qualities which above all include an ability for dealing with people, both publicly and individually, and resilience, mental and physical. Because the work defies slick or concise definition, there is also the fascination of knowing that the moment when one can lean back and say "Now I have mastered it" will never arrive. The theatre quickly reflects social atmosphere and change, both in its own products and in the attitude of its public, and this alone means constant adjustment, fore-thoughtfulness and an ever-burning fire of new ideas. It is not enough to be with it; one should be thinking and planning a jump ahead.

Putting it briefly, the ultimate purpose of theatre management is to create conditions as nearly ideal as possible in which the production side may have the best showing, and in which the audience may be predisposed, by the attention to their well-being, to enjoy what they have come to see.

A wise manager learns to choose as heads of all departments those whom he can trust and who can take responsibility for the activities within their special provinces. The ability to delegate is of prime importance. An efficiently run and pleasant theatre is very much a collective effort, which explains its fascination and its satisfaction for those who work in it.

No manager is expected to be a complete Jack-of-all-trades in the theatre, particularly in these days of managerial and technical development, but the more he knows about all its aspects the better for him and for the theatre. He will have sufficient know-how to choose good staff from whom he will not ask the absurd or the impossible. He will know when the last straw will break the back of even the most docile and hard-working camels backstage. He will above all command the respect as well as the liking which will keep him out of labour troubles and create the will to work throughout the theatre. Willy-nilly, he is the focus of activity and the initiator of it, the scapegoat, the buffer state, and he must accept the fact that he could well have in his office the famous motto that "the buck stops here" since all bucks will inevitably find their way to him.

These preoccupations in his own theatre could well occupy all a manager's time and attention, but if they are to be purposeful he must be able to lift his head from the daily round to take cognizance of what is happening in the wider theatre world and its relation to the community. Tides ebb and flow very quickly in the world today, of which he must be quick to take advantage, to take his own theatre on to fortune away from the shallows and the miseries which can claim it all too quickly.

Those of us in the theatre who have learnt from experience owe more than can be expressed to those who bore with us and patiently instructed us, both by example and advice, and best of all, worked with us. This is the moment for me to name some of the organizations to which I owe so much pleasure, instruction and gratitude for both—the management of H. M. Tennent, especially in the days of the Company of Four at the Lyric Theatre, Hammersmith, and to the staff in that theatre; Glyndebourne Opera; the English Opera Group and its focus of operation, the Aldeburgh Festival of Music and the Arts, the joint management of which enlarged my horizons and experience more than I could ever have hoped for; currently the Oxford Playhouse, whose inherited tradition is now extended as the Oxford University Theatre. My friends and colleagues in all these are too numerous to name, and their contribution to my ideals of management too valuable and too varied to be circumscribed in any form of written acknowledgement. Finally, deepest gratitude to Percy Corry, an untiring and meticulous editor, ever ready to guide me through the labyrinth.

Books could be written on many of the topics raised all too cursorily in this brief compass, and the lapse of time between writing and publication makes omissions all too apparent. For such inadequacies I apologize and can only hope this book will be used as a pointer rather than a primer.

ELIZABETH SWEETING

# ACKNOWLEDGMENTS

The author wishes to express her thanks to the following for permission to reproduce photographs included in this book: Plate I, Dennis Wompra, photographer; II, *The Architectural Review* (photographer Felicia Cronin); III, Arthur Winter, photographer; IV, Peter Moro & Partners (photographer John Donat); V, Maurice Broomfield, photographer; VI, Denys Lasdun & Partners (photographer Robert Kirkman); VII, Chichester Festival Theatre (photographer David Cole); VIII, Elsom, Mann & Cooper Ltd., Photographers.

# TWO VOICES

## 1895

"Theatrical management in this country is one of the most desperate commercial forms of gambling. . . . You must disturb a man's reason before he will even listen to a proposal to run a playhouse."

George Bernard Shaw: Preface to *The Theatrical "World" of 1894*
by William Archer (London, Walter Scott, Ltd.)


## 1965

"What constitutes a good manager in this field? He has been described by an authority on the subject as a man 'who must be knowledgeable in the art with which he is concerned, an impresario, labour negotiator, diplomat, educator, publicity and public relations expert, politician, skilled businessman, a social sophisticate, a servant of the community, a tireless leader—becomingly humble before authority—a teacher, a tyrant, and a continuing student of the arts.' "

*The Performing Arts: Problems and Prospects.*
Rockefeller Panel Report on the future of
theatre, dance, music in America.

# CONTENTS

## ILLUSTRATIONS
(Between pages 114 and 115)

*Part One*
The Pattern of
Theatre and Related Arts

# I

## THE PATTERN OF THEATRE AND RELATED ARTS IN BRITAIN

ALTHOUGH this is not the appropriate place for a full-scale discussion of the vicissitudes and achievements of British theatre, the scope within which basic management principles and practice have to be applied should be at least briefly indicated. The great strength of the theatres in Britain is that they have individuality within their categories and the would-be manager must detect and interpret this.

Early in this century, metropolitan theatre concentrated in London would have been the only activity worth discussing. Now the geographical distribution is much wider. While London's West End remains the Mecca for many people, there are now few regions in Britain which are not within reach of a theatre of some kind, and the kinds are many and varied. The repertory theatre, the civic theatre, the university theatre, arts centres and arts associations all serve in their different ways the communities in which they are situated and often a wider area over the surrounding counties in these days of increasing car ownership. They usually have room also for that peculiarly British activity, amateur drama, which is often of a very high standard and well worth including in the year's programme. All these kinds make different demands on their administration.

There is also a wider division which is useful for practical purposes of description, into the subsidized and non-subsidized theatre, i.e. that which receives and depends largely upon money received from outside sources to augment the box-office receipts, and that which uses the money of its commercial promoters and their backers. These two divisions are sometimes also termed "non-commercial" and "commercial," but unfortunately these are often used, wrongly, with a connotation on the one hand of something likely to appeal only to a minority and likely to fail in a financial sense, and on the other, performed for profit and liable to be deemed unlikely to have great artistic merit. Neither of these suppositions is wholly correct but the factual description, "subsidized" and "non-subsidized," seems to avoid such connotations.

It also cuts across geographical divisions. London's West End is the hub of non-subsidized theatre and the home of the managements who control the theatres. London is also the home of the National Theatre, the Royal Opera House, with the Royal Ballet under the same roof, and the other "national" companies, Sadler's Wells Opera and a special section of the Royal Shakespeare Company domiciled there as well as in Stratford-upon-Avon. All these national companies receive subsidy from the Arts Council of Great Britain. So also does the Royal Court Theatre, founded by George Devine primarily as the theatre for new dramatists—among them John Osborne, Arnold Wesker and Ann Jellicoe—and some experimental groups in London, such as the Arts Laboratory which is a unique hive of activity and exploration in new forms. At a recent count, it was said that the number of theatres which will be licensed by the Greater London Council (since the juris-diction of the Lord Chamberlain has ceased) is 31 in the West End, and 19 in the London area outside the West End, with 23 premises in the West End and 22 in other parts of London licensed annually for stage plays.

Outside London, one thinks first of the repertory theatres, i.e. theatres presenting for most of the year a programme of plays by a resident company. There are variations on this theme. Not all these theatres keep the same companies for the whole season; some retain a nucleus, recruiting their extra actors as and when required for particular plays. All of them are designed to serve their particular area and receive subsidy from the Arts Council for this purpose. Some also tour to other repertory theatres, university and civic theatres and occasionally to other theatres which receive only touring com-panies. This movement around the country is a very stimu-lating recent development, making new demands on the actors who confront different audiences and varying the staple fare for the audiences. Some theatres for particular reasons operate only seasonally with a resident company but like to have visiting attractions. The organization of these manifold requirements offers great variety to a manager and has its own form of administration.

Management of theatres in the provinces has now acquired very much greater responsibility by reason of the subsidy received. Grants from the Arts Council are often the main source of subsidy, but local authorities, encouraged by the Arts Council and by the Government through Miss Jennie Lee, Minister for the Arts, also give substantial sums. Local industry may also contribute, particularly to arts centres and arts associations, and charitable foundations also contribute, as does the Arts Council from a special fund, to capital expenditure on buildings and equipment. The budgeting and use of what are now large sums of money coming from outside sources involve a very much more complex administrative set-up and control than was needed when repertory theatres operated on a much more modest scale, dependent mainly on the box-office from well-tried West End successes after the rights became generally available rather than the handsome productions of classical plays and the hazard of new plays which they now all include in their programmes. There is no question that public taste has expanded to expect higher standards of acting and presentation and a more exacting and adventurous range of plays. The Arts Council and all other bodies concerned to make theatre available to as great a number of people as possible take cognizance of this and endeavour to foster this advance by bridging the gap between the large amounts of money which are needed and the limited box-office take from comparatively small buildings, holding usually about 1,000 or fewer, and prices which are within the spending power of all.

The non-subsidized companies are also an important source of the life-blood of the provinces. Not only do they present plays in London but they have a long tradition of touring in the big theatres which exist in most of the principal towns all over Britain. These tours may be prior to the West End run or after it and they augment the work of the regional theatres by showing to the audience the star performers, the large-scale musical or large-cast play, which is outside the scope of the repertory theatres. The story of touring is not, alas, so happy a one as that of the repertory theatre. The cost of touring has soared, many of the touring theatres are large and, having been built to serve a more opulent age, when repertory theatres were fewer, are uneconomical to run. Consequently, good tours have become more rare, since managers cannot risk heavy losses, and audiences have dropped away, creating the vicious circle in which not even the best and most publicized shows can always cover costs. This is a great blow to the theatre in general, since it whittles away all the time the potential theatre-going audience on whom we all depend, and it is serious indeed if the provinces are to be deprived of so much that is good. It may well be that the present allocation of subsidy may in some way be extended to include what the so-called commercial theatre has to offer, to the eventual benefit of both the theatre world and the general public. The present Committee of Enquiry set up by the Arts Council may well come to some such conclusion, bearing in mind Lord Goodman's prefatory note to *A New Charter*, the twenty-second annual report (1967) of the Arts Council, of which he is Chairman, in the course of which he says—

> The English theatre flourished under private management before we were dreamed of. It is our duty in the administration of subsidy to co-operate with the best elements. Whether we can or should in the end give direct aid to private managements is a problem we are now investigating.

The subsidized national companies based in London also do their share of touring, so that their work is not exclusively for London. As this is regarded as an essential part of their work, the extra cost is reflected in their subsidy, but the problems are basically the same as for any other touring company. Some are practically solved by, for example, the provision of specially designed vans for transporting a repertoire of productions and for storing the sets and costumes when space in the theatres is inadequate, but others are being tackled by a new plan of operation. In 1967, the National Theatre, The Royal Opera and Ballet, the Royal Shakespeare Company and Sadler's Wells Opera, formed the Dramatic and Lyric Theatres Association, DALTA, to stay in selected theatres of appropriate size and facilities over a long period. A brochure issued for one such season puts the advantages very succinctly—

A theatrical feast which could not have been envisaged under former touring arrangements. Freed from the rigours which are part and parcel of "one-week stands" they will be able to devote more time to rehearsal and consequently to the establishment of a broader and more interesting repertory.

The scheme will also be of immeasurable benefit to the artists themselves, who, no longer required to live temporary, "out-of-suitcase" existences, will be able to settle down to routines similar to those experienced when working in their own theatres. The potential gains—a heightening of their morale and the maintenance of a high standard of performance.

Above all else, DALTA will bring to you an unprecedented opportunity for discriminating and selective theatre-going, hitherto impossible outside London.

DALTA plans to increase the number of companies in the group, which will spread its benefits even more widely to its members and its audiences. This type of co-ordination may well be a pointer for the future and at present is a boon to many a harassed manager in the provinces who finds a sizeable chunk of time filled with a properly co-ordinated programme of a high standard, rather than a random selection juxtaposing good and mediocre.

If this gives an impression that theatre in Britain eludes categories, is constantly intermingling and developing, that is right. It is a sign of vigorous life in which playwrights, actors, production staff and managers all have demanding work if they are to take the tide at the flood. The omens are good, but only as good as the individuals who will take full advantage of them. The repertory theatres have a flying start and more money behind them than ever before. Non-subsidized companies are reaching out to new plays by new authors and revivals of the classics. While the National Theatre waits for its new home on the South Bank, it goes on enlarging its repertoire and going out with the other national companies to the provinces. Meanwhile there are other signs of life and development and some of these need more exploration to show how the tentacles of theatre are reaching out in the community everywhere.

# 2

## CIVIC THEATRES

THE attitude of civic authorities to the arts has been under-going a radical change. There is a feeling of obligation and a desire to provide the facilities for those who wish to develop their imaginative world, to open the windows, even though only a minority may look out at first.

There are two main ways of providing theatre under civic companies. Many of our established repertory companies owe their buildings to the initiative of the civic authority, among them Coventry's Belgrade Theatre, the Nottingham Playhouse, and the Phoenix Theatre, Leicester. These house permanent repertory companies, providing under the same management a planned programme of professional theatre for most of the year. They usually have a permanent administration with a resident Artistic Director. Financial arrangements *vis-à-vis* the local authority are complex and varied. The company may be autonomous, choosing plays and mounting them on budgets approved by a Board on which the local authority is repre-sented, and paying a rent to the authority. They may have no responsibility for the maintenance of the fabric—another form of contribution made by the authority to help the general running costs. In other cases the theatre staff may be direct employees of the authority, retaining a measure of responsibility for artistic policy and the running of the theatre. Yet again, the local authority may be one of several patrons.

The deciding factor in setting up a theatre is the degree and the kind of local demand. Some communities are large enough to have sufficient potential theatre-goers to fill a theatre nearly all the time, if not to capacity, at least to a level of box office providing adequate income when receipts and subsidy are combined. Others, for manifold reasons—small size, situation in a sparsely populated catchment area, seasonal or holiday

activity only, to cite a few—cannot sustain a professional programme for the whole year.

This brings us to the second main category of civic theatre,
which has been so well described in the Arts Council's 20th
Annual Report 1964–5 (pages 27–8)—

> . . . there has come into being a new type of public theatre—
> the Civic Theatre, as it has come to be called—which is not
> committed to any one particular type of policy (as, for in-
> stance, a resident repertory or touring theatre), but attempts
> to present a mixed programme of events, to suit the varied
> interests of theatre-going folk in the area. So, in any one
> year in these theatres, there may be a period of visiting
> touring companies followed by a repertory season, followed
> in turn by pantomime, and amateur attractions; and inter-
> spersed with these there may be concerts, jazz sessions,
> poetry recitals, art exhibitions and film shows. This is "The
> Theatre As a Civic Arts Centre" intended to provide for
> the needs of all age groups and open during the day as well
> as at night; sensible plans are being made to link them all
> together in a loose association (National Council of Civic
> Theatres) for the planning of programmes and co-ordinating
> of tours.

A project of this kind necessitates an elaborate building and
naturally, with all the other demands on the ratepayers'
money and the competition for priority, progress on this ideal
scale is not rapid.

The Civic Theatre is really the focus of the regional association for the arts which Miss Jennie Lee hailed as the hope for
the future in the famous White Paper of February 1965, *A
Policy for the Arts, The first Steps*—

> Some of our new civic centres and arts centres already demon-
> strate that an agreeable environment and a jealous regard
> for the maintenance of high standards are not incompatible.
> Centres that succeed in providing a friendly meeting ground
> where light entertainment and cultural projects can be en-
> joyed help also to break down the isolation from which both
> artist and potential audience have suffered in the past.

We must not imagine that all is rosy or an easy progress towards such a cultural Utopia. At present many enlightened civic authorities have either built and subsidized theatres or theatre companies, or taken an existing flourishing concern into what could be described as protective custody. Places so diverse as Bristol, Crewe, Sunderland, Hull, Norwich, Watford, Bradford, Birmingham, and York to name only a few, all act in some manner for their theatres. A major act of rescue has occurred in Bury St. Edmunds, where the Theatre Royal, of unique architectural importance and restored by private effort to something of its original character of 1819, is a going concern with a mixed programme, including local amateurs, with the help of the East Suffolk County Council and several Borough, Urban and Rural District Councils. Bristol has a regional Arts Centre and Arts Centres are projected in many other places.

The authorities who are beginners at the theatrical game have to avoid one great temptation in this day and age where support of the arts has its own *réclame*. They must not regard a theatre as a status symbol and build one for the sheer hell of it, for hell it will in that case surely be. The basic question is "What should our theatre provide for local demands and requirements?" Only when policy has been realistically assessed and defined can one brick be laid on another with any hope of a future for the theatre, its owners and its users.

The reluctance of local authorities even to use a minor part of the permission of Section 132 of the Local Government Act of 1948 save for a 6d. rate for the provision of entertainment is well-known and discouraging. The expenditure on cultural activities is still a small percentage of expenditure on entertainment as a whole. It has been alliteratively said that not all authorities like "the idea of paying for Bartok and Brecht out of the Bingo."

Even so, the move is in the right direction. The mixed programme of the civic theatre may not please all the people all the time, but will cater for many of the people most of the time. As Shaw says, to many "the higher drama is as disagreeably perplexing as the game of chess is to a man who has barely enough capacity to understand skittles." But, he goes on, "We have the chess club and the skittle alley prospering side by side." That was in 1891. Perhaps by 1991 we shall have many and prosperous theatres where entertainments so diverse all flourish.

## THE MANAGEMENT OF A CIVIC THEATRE

Theatre is so specialized an activity that it cannot be placed in the same category as some other amenities under the council's umbrella. If the authority decides to have a permanent company, the artistic policy, supported by realistic and efficient business control, is finally the core of the enterprise. Everything will depend on the choice of play and the standard of production. These are matters which cannot be left to a civil or municipal servant because they all call for a know-how, a background and experience only to be gained in the professional theatre. An act of faith is required for any council embarking on a hazard as open to public criticism as the theatre to hand over the responsibility for it to someone outside its own sphere, but in fact this should be done. The Artistic Director, shadowed by a professional theatre administrator, is the key figure. He may be answerable to a Board or body representing local interests, including local amateur drama, in which the local council may well have overruling voting power, but he must be allowed to work in his own world independently to achieve the policy. Budgets and the actual financial results will be the concern of the City or Borough Treasurer, but when the choice of the key staff has been made, mutual trust must be the aim of both parties. Only then will the theatre have a constructive image, suited for its community, instead of a nationalized blue-print at worst. The Institute of Municipal Entertainment organizes an examination for managers for their theatres which should produce managers of a calibre and with the knowledge to ensure the success of this side.

No civic authority need feel itself lonely in establishing a theatre or supporting a company. Advice is always available from the Arts Council, and indeed there is usually an early impulse to explore the possibility of combining Arts

Council and municipal subsidy. The Theatres' Advisory
Council exists for this very purpose and held in 1965 a very
interesting conference with the Association of Municipal
Corporations.

There is also a National Council for Civic Theatres, inaugurated in 1964 by the initiative of Reginald Birks, Director of the
Sunderland Empire. It aims at the development of a chain
of municipally owned theatres and the setting up of special
productions which will tour them. Much remains to be
done in this scheme, and there are, of course, manifold difficulties to be overcome. Its significance is that this new field for
touring and its operation in the professional theatre are being
explored on the one hand; on the other, it signals the aware-
ness and eagerness of local authorities to set up and fill new
theatres built for up-to-date requirements.

Much more could and should be written on this lively new
branch of theatre activity. Suffice it here to close with a note
of warning. The decision to build a theatre does not end with
the completion of the bricks and mortar. It is the beginning
of a long history of occasional profit, frequent loss and constant
hazard. No authority should forget that the theatre will
never swell the coffers all the time. Constant and probably
increasing subsidy is essential, the more so as the project
succeeds and gathers momentum, if standards are to be maintained and raised.

Nigel Abercrombie, then Secretary-General of the Arts
Council, spoke on this point to the 1964 Conference of the
Local Authorities to consider the Survey of Municipal Enter-
tainment in England and Wales 1947–48 and 1961–62.

> Cultural entertainment is a money-loser. This is not to the
> discredit of humanity. It is a simple matter of arithmetic.
> The highest standards of quality are necessarily a minority
> interest, but audiences must represent majorities if perform-
> ances are to pay for themselves. There is no compelling
> reason I know, no moral obligation, for local authorities to
> spend money on any cultural entertainment at all, but two
> points do stand out; if they do spend money on cultural
> entertainment they will lose it, but if they don't they will
> soon be sorry for it.

REFERENCES

Because development in civic theatre is so rapid and so various reports become quickly out of date, but the following documents referred to in the text, may be of use.

*A Survey of Municipal Entertainment in England and Wales* (Institute of Municipal Entertainment, obtainable from John Burton, White Rock Pavilion, Hastings, Sussex. Price 10s. 6d.)

"An Essay Towards the Civic Theatre" by Hugh Jenkins (Chairman of the Standing Advisory Council on Local Authorities and the Theatre) in *Essays in Local Government Enterprise* (Merlin Press. Price 15s.)

*National Council for Civic Theatres Survey* 1964–5 (NCCT, obtainable from the Civic Theatre, Sunderland. Price 15s.)

*The Theatre and the Local Authority.* A survey issued by the Department of Adult Education, the University of Hull and the Yorkshire North District of the W.E.A. It was prepared by students of a tutorial class in drama in association with their tutor, Miss Muriel Crane.

Bulletins issued by the Theatres' Advisory Council, 9 Fitzroy Square, London, W.1.

*Theatres in the Regions.* Issues arising from the four Regional Meetings on Theatre and the Local Authorities, prepared in September, 1968 by the Standing Advisory Committee on Local Authorities and the Theatre.

# 3

## ARTS CENTRES, ARTS ASSOCIATIONS AND FESTIVALS

THESE, though very disparate in character, are taken under one heading because they consist in a complex of the arts, of which a theatre is often the focus.

### THE ARTS CENTRE

There are as yet comparatively few of these in existence, though many are on the drawing board because they are being increasingly thought of as a magnet for the leisure interests of the community. To find a prototype for the elaborate arts centre we must look to France, where André Malraux, head of the Ministry for Cultural Affairs set up in 1959, determined to spread the availability of the arts and recreation into the provinces. The Maison de la Culture in France provides under one roof one or more theatres, usually a large one for opera and ballet and a smaller one for drama, a cinema, art gallery, reading room, cafeteria, etc., all at reasonable cost to their users as contrasted with the astronomical costs of those amenities in the capital. Twenty-one were planned but there are as yet fewer than a dozen because of the vicissitudes of the Government and local subsidy, but those which have been successfully set up are providing what they promised. Bourges can be cited as a notable example where plays, concerts, ballet, art and poetry have a patronage of about 11,500 ticket-holders in the population of 65,000.

The Maisons de la Culture achieve another important purpose by stabilizing the chosen base of a flourishing theatre company, which serves the region as well as the town.

The situation in Britain is not quite comparable. We already have regional theatres with a long tradition and it would not necessarily be the answer to rehouse them in an elaborate building along with other activities. Perhaps the nearest we have is the proposed scheme for the Barbican, with its juxtaposition of a theatre, premises for the Guildhall School of Music and Drama, a concert hall and amenities common to all with special provision for the work of each. The other pioneer project, a sensation of 1968, is the Billingham Forum. This town of 35,000 population has now under the same roof, a 2,500-seater concert hall interchangeable as an ice-skating rink, a 675-seat theatre, used by a professional repertory company and convertible to a cinema; together with facilities for squash, indoor bowling, three sports halls and a crèche for the children while their parents sample these delights. All this in a busy town centre and easily accessible. Its brochure claims that it is "aimed to become not only the recreational and artistic centre of Teeside but to set up a pattern for the future in modern entertainment facilities."

Let us hope that it will indeed do this. Not all centres will be like Bourges or Billingham, but they can work to the same purpose. Those who wish for them must go out and find potential customers and work up the necessary enthusiasm. Equally important is the need to continue to stimulate the need and the interest—which may be so latent as to be hardly discernible —by supplying work of the highest possible standard in the building when they have been achieved. It is here that the Arts Associations can help.

## THE ARTS ASSOCIATION

This may be defined as a confederation of local authorities, industrial and other organizations and interested individuals concerned to stimulate, develop and sponsor activities concerned with all the arts in a particular region. The Northern Arts Association, formed in 1961, is a prototype. It is financed from a portion of the rates by local authorities and other members—local firms, clubs, societies, and individuals— pay what they can afford, with a minimum of five guineas.

Tours to the theatres and halls of the region by professional theatre, ballet and opera companies are promoted, exhibitions are arranged and the magazine of the Association encourages local writers. It is a good pattern and flexible in that artistic events are helped by whatever means are appropriate and practical, such as advice, professional guidance, finance, publicity or transport. Some funds are available from national sources via the Arts Council and some national trusts also contribute. The aim is to display over the area the best examples available in all the arts and to avoid the duplication or concentration in a few places which individual planning may produce. There is a very informative section on this topic in the Annual Report of the Arts Council for 1965–6, *Key Year*, with some figures indicative of the spending in the NEAA area.

The involvement of many interests in the Arts Association is an acceptable idea to those who contribute to the finance. The whole community benefits by having a more interesting and varied bill of fare than separate managements could produce, and those places which have a few facilities are provided with something either their own limited premises or within reachable distance.

In spite of setbacks and inherent difficulties, it is nevertheless quite clear that the setting up of more regional arts associations will eventually be of enormous benefit to all the arts. The question of suitable premises may be partially solved by the increased number of civic theatres planned and the general interchange of companies, exhibitions and artists will become easier when there are more of these bodies to handle it. Already in the Arts Council report for the year ended 31 March 1967, the list of Arts Centres and Arts Associations, large like the NEAA, and involved with the local authority or the many smaller ones which do not have local authority help, is very impressive indeed in number and geographical distribution.

## FESTIVALS

The implication of the term "festival" needs a little clarification and indeed warning. The festival, judging by the lists of so-called festivals in many programmes of forthcoming events, seems to have become a favourite national sport. In the sense that the term implies a pleasurable occasion, and something special, this is good. But far too often the term is applied to any conglomeration of events strung together without any particular link or purpose. It is also used, some say bitterly, like the term "gala performance," as an excuse to charge inflated prices.

A festival proper should be open to none of these derogatory comments. It should spring from the genuine desire to co-ordinate a number of diverse activities and entertainments, each one of the highest possible standard, to create a unique entity or to illuminate and explore a particular theme. Such an example is the Festival of Music and the Arts held in Alde-burgh, Suffolk, initiated in 1948 by Benjamin Britten in this small East Anglian fishing town with a population of about 3,000, at first sight an unpromising milieu, ill-provided with the physical facilities for the chamber opera, concerts, exhi-bitions and lectures which were proposed. The Bath Festival has been similarly established and enriched by the presiding genius of Yehudi Menuhin over a period of years. At the other end of the spectrum from tiny Aldeburgh on the East Coast is the capital city, Edinburgh, and its International Festival, which is among the most famous in the world. It displays annually great companies, orchestras and individuals which can be seen in Britain only on this occasion, and turns Edin-burgh into the most cosmopolitan of cities with its performers and its audience. Pitlochry is a focus of good drama in the heart of one of the most beautiful areas of Scotland and provides a season of varied and attractive entertainment in civilized surroundings for the multitudes who take their holidays there.

All these have something unique and strong enough to draw big audiences from all over the place. As well as having the official Festival events, they stimulate the participation of other activities "on the fringe," so that the visitor has an *embarras de richesse* to enjoy. There is thus an authentically festive atmosphere and a unified artistic purpose, so that every-thing has a stamp of excellence upon it. Comparison of the true festival with a haphazard *ad hoc* collection of events must show that the one is as different from the other as chalk from cheese.

THE ADMINISTRATION OF FESTIVALS, ARTS ASSOCIA-
TIONS AND ARTS CENTRES

There is no more interesting and complex job than that of
the administrator of these organizations, and rather special
qualities are required. His personal qualities must be those
which make a good manager in any sphere—a talent for clear
and efficient organization, a paramount ability to work with
and through committees and the officials of worlds other than
his own, and an ability to understand and cope with the whole
range of human frailty from the greatest prima donna to the
newest and youngest stage hand.

The Administrator of any co-ordination of the arts will
find that he must acquire the know-how of each one of these.
He must understand the special requirements and idiosyncrasies of musicians, the spacing of their rehearsal and
performance time, how to deal with music publishers and
performing rights, the intricacies of their contracts and the
discipline of the Musicians' Union. For the visual arts, there
are the requirements of space and lighting in exhibition premises, the transport and insurance terms, supervision and security.
Poetry recitals demand special knowledge of copyright and
reproduction rights. He will be faced with the design and printing of the vast programme and also with the collection of
materials, notes on the works performed, photographs, advertisements, etc. Every event must have its adequate rehearsal time
allowed, and many a Festival manager has fallen into the trap
at some time or other of having too many groups seeking too few
places and overlapping rehearsals and performances! He must
have a clear programme for the domestic detail—the removal
of a piano from a concert in time to allow the same stage to be
used for ballet, the continuous tuning of keyboard instruments,
the setting up and timely removal of chairs—all the minute
detail which can be taken for granted as done and overlooked,
so that chaos is come again.

In an Arts Association and Arts Centre the empire is far-
flung. It is essential that the administrator should know his
area and the key personnel in local authorities and organizations. He must be a good committee man and a diplomat,
able quickly to assess the value of a project and to translate it

into practical and financial terms. He must be a walking calendar of dates and events and avoid having important events in the area in competition with instead of following each other. Like the Festival manager, he must have artistic perception of the balance of the programme so that the emphasis does not lie too heavily in any one direction. He must be a wizard with accounts. Festival and Arts Association finances are by no means as straightforward as those for a theatre. The raising of money and the control of subsidy are his constant concern, and above all, he must always be thinking ahead, looking for ways of future expansion, assessing needs and anticipating them.

There is much useful advice in the pamphlet, *Notes of Guidance in the Formation of a Regional Arts Association,* prepared by Raymond Aitchison (Lincolnshire Association), Alexander Dunbar (Northern Arts Association) and Eric White (Arts Council of Great Britain), after discussion with the Department of Education and Science.

Arts Centres are a comparatively recent phenomenon. Indeed the Centre at Basildon, Essex, opened in 1968, and serving a population in the district of about 80,000, is described by Lord Goodman in a message printed in its brochure as "the first Arts Centre specially designed and tailored for all its functions since the war." It has a multipurpose auditorium for use as a theatre, cinema or exhibition area, with concomitant facilities such as restaurant, bars, administrative offices, projection room, committee rooms, etc. The increasingly wide provision for leisure pursuits is reflected in its studios for pottery, painting, sculpture and photography. Another interesting example is that in Corby, Northamptonshire, which is a prize-winning civic centre including a swimming-pool and adjoining council administrative block. Billingham Forum is yet another notable complex.

These are patterns for the future for which managers with experience of a full range of arts administration will be increasingly in demand. Such centres can, if well-planned and deployed over the country to fulfil regional needs, provide a focus for the arts and all leisure pursuits. To new towns with no tradition of such activity they can provide an invaluable social and artistic stimulus.

# 4

## THE THEATRE AND
## YOUNG PEOPLE

UNLIKE many of the European countries, notably Russia and Sweden, we have no tradition of theatres for children, i.e. special plays professionally performed by companies of actors in theatres designated for this purpose. It is only recently that serious attention has been paid to the other facet of theatre for young people, a close link between young people and the professional theatre for which provision is made as a part of the regular programme. It is truly amazing that Inner London has only one theatre, the Arts, permanently catering for children and that the child is often brought thus to associate the theatre with Christmas only. At the time of writing, the National Theatre has a project afoot to set up a young people's theatre on a site not far from its present habitat in the Waterloo Road. This is still a far cry from the status accorded to children's theatre in other countries, but it could set a hall-mark on this genre by giving it National Theatre status.

But the picture is changing and improving. The small number of companies who have been bold and courageous enough to struggle on with their tours of plays for children are now receiving encouragement, the possibility of financial aid and recognition of their value. Professional theatre companies in the provinces are stretching out their influence into the schools and, most significant fact of all, they are being welcomed and encouraged to do so.

The reasons for the change of heart do not lie entirely in the theatre. They lie in the same dawning idea of the place of the arts in the community which is leading local authorities to want to build theatres. Among the arts drama is now recognized as playing a vital part. The Ministry of Education's report, *Half Our Future* (1963), admirably summarizes this—

Drama can offer something more significant than the day-dream. It helps boys and girls to identify themselves with men and women of whom they have heard or read. By playing out psychologically significant situations, they can work out their own personal problems. Here is one way in which they can be helped to reconcile the reality of the world outside with their own private worlds. Once this begins, education has something on which to build.

This new attention to the use of drama as what might be called a therapy is evident in teaching methods for subjects other than drama and in the extensive use, for instance, of improvisation to bring school work to life. The use of dramatic method and material in plays to liberate and stabilize is now expertly employed. This is a fascinating world, but, belonging as it does to teaching methods rather than to the theatre proper, it must be relinquished in this particular context.

More significant for the present purpose, as a guide-line from education to drama *per se* is another comment from the same report—

It is a matter of some concern that the educative experience of drama in all its forms is too often, despite notable exceptions, restricted or denied to pupils. In school, the reason is often lack of suitable teachers or accommodation; outside, in many areas, there are far too few opportunities for seeing high-quality productions in the theatre. The stimulation of interest in the professional theatre, and encouragement to feel that it is part of their own, not an alien, culture, is particularly important for the older boys and girls, if they are not to miss this source of enrichment of their adult lives.

Written five years ago, this wistful comment on the distance between school and theatre is much less true today, but may well have done much to create the climate of thought in which the two worlds have drawn closer, to the advantage of both.

While in the world of education there has been a new evaluation of the arts, the theatre has had its own change of heart.

It would be invidious to single out many separate names among the provincial subsidized theatres now running schemes for children. They include Coventry, Oxford, Sheffield,

Colchester, Salisbury and others. Plans are no longer restricted
to the schools matinée—too often in the theatre of the past an
easy way of boosting the box office and for the children a
welcome break from routine. There are days spent in the
working theatre, watching actors rehearse, studying the work-
shops for scenery and costumes, examining and using the stage
equipment, having discussions with the actors, directors and
designers. Children now learn what goes on behind the stage
and come to regard the theatre as a place for the co-ordination
of many different creative gifts and acquired expertise as well
as for the magic of performance.

Sometimes the spearhead of the theatre comes to the schools.
Specially trained actors visit the schools with scenes from current plays and use the children themselves to perform and
improvise. The old passivity of "watching a play" has gone,
and its place is being taken by the eagerness of youngsters in
the schools to become the informed and critical audience of
the future, who will expect and recognize high standards of
performance. Nothing but good can come from all this, an
extension of pleasure for the adult-to-be and an audience of
the future to keep the theatre on its toes. Nor do the children
now believe that the theatre is only Shakespeare, and the plays
set for examinations at that. They are encouraged to see plays
of a much wider range, from the Greeks to John Osborne.


CHILDREN'S THEATRE COMPANIES

Some far-sighted theatre people, sympathetic to children,
have been operating special companies to perform to children.
Among them, Caryl Jenner and Brian Way could not be
omitted in any survey, however cursory. Caryl Jenner's Uni-
corn Theatre is now settled in the Arts Theatre and Brian Way's
Theatre Centre in Willesden does a magnificent job of touring
to schools with special programmes and of running a hive of
varied activity in its own building. It also plans to build
research studios on a site in Redbridge with accommodation
for courses. Michael Croft's National Youth Theatre has a
national and international reputation. He uses school children
and undergraduates in productions of Shakespeare and the

classics, touring in Britain and abroad, and sometimes having a season in a London theatre, so that he covers a great range of audiences to great effect. A report has been issued, entitled "Youth Theatre," by David Wright, expressing the hope that in time every town will have its own Youth Theatre with the encouragement of local authorities.

A great achievement for permanent children's theatre outside London is John English's Midland Arts Centre in Birmingham, set up on land leased from the City and catering for the ages of 5 to 25 in a variety of buildings and plays. In 1967 this first permanent and professional theatre for young people announced that it hoped to increase by ten times the number of people attending the theatre in the Birmingham area. In its small studio theatre, holding 186, it not only organizes and presents drama but imparts the essential know-how and behaviour. The enterprise goes from strength to strength.

Naturally one would wish for all children the experience of seeing a performance in its rightful setting of the theatre, but the basic experience, the community of actors and audience, can be achieved to a remarkable degree in a school hall or classroom.

Young people will soon be more familiar with what drama is, by reason of the new approach to it such as is outlined in a Schools Council paper published in 1968, *Humanities for the young school-leaver—an approach through English* (H. M. Stationery Office). Drama and poetry are thought of as a major channel of experience—

> Presentation by pupils of their individual and group experience is seen as an essential part, and some examples are given of the form this might take, and the creative skills and techniques it can bring out.

If young people do this, they will be awakened to the whole world of human relationships in which drama consists and of which the theatre illustrates the significance.

All the ways of bringing young people into the mainstream of theatre may benefit from the recent Young People's Theatre Enquiry, set up by the Arts Council in 1965, with a report issued on its findings entitled *The Provision of Theatre for Young People in Great Britain*. The committee received evidence and

collected information from countless sources and visited notable
organizations such as the Midland Arts Centre and the Theatre
in Education team of the Belgrade Theatre, Coventry. The
initial and perhaps most important result may be that financial
help will be forthcoming for theatre for young people in this
country. If this can be deployed in imaginative ways, as well
as in lump sums to theatre companies, there are no limits to
the benefits which should accrue from this investigation and
from the stimulus it will give to all who care about this branch
of theatre life and energy.

A national survey of educational drama was also launched
by H.M. Inspectorate and carried out between September 1966
and Easter 1967. John Allen, writing of this in *Trends in Education* (January, 1967; H.M.S.O. publication: Department of
Education and Science, price 3s. 6d.) explains that it is to be
done with "the collaboration of local authority inspectors,
county drama inspectors, county drama advisers, youth organizers and others" and will "attempt to establish the place of
drama in schools, its contribution to education and its relationship to other subjects." The findings are now published in
*Drama* (published by the Department of Education and Science,
price 9s. 6d.).

Two such massive projects need no more comment to empha-
size the importance given today to drama and young people,
and their findings and recommendations could have incal-
culably far-reaching results. Information is being exchanged
in the regions. A Conference on Young People and the Theatre,
organized by the Northern Arts Association and held in
Billingham Forum in November 1968, was the first of what is
hoped may be a series of regional conferences on Young
People and the Arts. The relation of the theatre with education
was examined in a conference on Drama and the Theatre in
Education held at Easter, 1969, in Bristol, sponsored by the
local Education Authority, Bristol Old Vic Company and
Clifton College.

# 5

## *THEATRE AND UNIVERSITY*

In April, 1965, there appeared in the national newspapers a brief announcement to the effect that the University of Lancaster was to receive £70,000 from the Nuffield Foundation to build a drama studio and workshop near the central hall of the University. There was a further comment that the studio would be used for experiments in drama rather than for public performances. Performances at the studio would not necessarily be part of the curriculum, although the University might offer some courses in drama in the future.

For those who are watching with interest signs of the growing recognition of theatre as a subject complex and respectable enough to be gathered into the University curriculum, this announcement was significant in many respects.

It summarized the present state of university theatre development: firstly, in the generous endowment from a Trust which has only recently shown interest in this field; secondly, in its clear distinction between the pressure and demands of public performances and those which explore and experiment for esoteric purposes; thirdly, the provision of special premises for the study of theatre, hopeful when too often it is relegated to the exigencies of an all-purpose hall; finally, the note of caution is sounded in the provision of related courses "in the future."

In most universities in Great Britain the status of dramatic activity is anomalous. Students spend a great deal of time producing plays, in the main without guidance about acting or production and in unsuitable *milieux*. Inevitably this extramural activity is frowned upon by many senior (i.e. faculty) members. The students continue to build up a tradition which is not professional (though it frequently aspires to reach this level) nor yet amateur in the sense that a local village society may happily put on an annual Gilbert and Sullivan or an old

West End success.  Much talent and experiment go into the
work and university actors and directors frequently progress
to the professional theatre.  This will always happen, given the
drive and initiative of potentially gifted men of the theatre who
can galvanize a whole vintage group.

It is curious, though, that this particular tributary of the professional theatre has to flow in obliquely.  Looking at it from
the point of view of the professional theatre, there is acknow-
ledged now to be room for the really gifted amateur to find his
way into it through these channels.  The distrust of the university background is less marked.  It has in fact much to offer to
the interpretation and direction of some plays and to the
originality of production and setting which an unconventional
director and designer can contribute.  So the comparatively
small number of university products in all these aspects of the
theatre is an active leaven.

The other factor necessary to the professional theatre is the
audience.  Undergraduates of all faculties can acquire a taste
and judgement about the theatre from a group or individuals
in their midst, indefatigably putting on production after production, often of plays rarely seen because no commercial
management would risk them, sometimes illuminating their
academic study by physical presentation of key works, sometimes giving shocks of pleasure, or simply shocks, by their
manner of visual staging.  Undergraduates who make up such
an audience may well continue to develop informed interest
after they have gone down.  At the same time, the university
(and one may include for this purpose the training college)
is often the link between school and the adult world, because
it is from it that teachers absorb their training and their
attitudes to the arts, which they impart in turn to the next
generation.

It is unlikely and probably not desirable for Britain to set
up anything like the systems of either the United States or the
continental countries since the theatre picture and the practical
finance are so different, but there are signs that theatre as a
complex of the arts is beginning to receive the academic recognition it deserves.  In comparison with the hours spent in
academic study, those devoted by undergraduates to "putting
on plays" bear a very high relation.  This alone should, in

the lowest terms, draw the attention of their mentors to the need for making this expense of effort more valuable. Since it is an activity which will never be abandoned, but is liable to expand and to consume even more time, a compromise should surely be sought by which it should be given recognition and increasing assistance.

The next step is to set up the necessary course which makes a department of drama. In part the resources already exist in literature and the arts, and there are potentially many courses valuable to other sides of the theatre which could be contributed from economics and social history, for instance, especially of the modern period. Pressures are increasing from the world outside towards the recognition of the usefulness of the arts and to the need to provide for them in a society where leisure is the goal, and where leisure is not just for loafing.

In all, this seems a moment when the universities are key points with much to contribute if the more farsighted of their authorities will show the imagination to grasp the chance. This means academic planning, setting up links with the professional theatre (theatre is finally connected with the stage rather than the study) spending money on staff and on adequate physical facilities in the new building areas and generally giving a blessing to the valuable activity which has so long flourished *sub rosa* and rather shamefacedly. And this is all beginning now to happen.

The first Drama Department in Britain was founded in 1946–47 at Bristol University. It offers the degree of B.A. Honours, either Special—a combination of the drama course with another subject based on a language or literature, or General—combined with special subjects or others not necessarily in a special school, such as Ancient History and Archaeology, the History of Music, or Philosophy. For the degrees of M.A. and Ph.D. the requirements are Theatre History of plays in performance, with a dissertation. Advanced practical theatre studies can lead to the postgraduate Certificate of Drama. They must include one session with the Bristol Old Vic's professional company and with the BBC, with two written papers. This requirement points to the strong links with the professional theatre, radio and TV which make the course particularly valuable for students aiming to enter the professional theatre,

while for the more academic course, many potential teachers
of drama in schools, there are equally close associations with
other departments in the Faculty of Arts, Music and Education.
   As well as working in the historic Theatre Royal, Bristol's
students have a studio theatre, small but practical, well-
equipped radio, film and TV studios, a workshop, and a theatre
collection. The *premières* of many plays by notable contemporary writers such as Pinter, Arden, Frisch and Obaldia have
taken place there, and encouragement is given to new writers
by the Play-writing Fellowship, which confers the benefit of
money and time to work in congenial surroundings and to
learn from seeing original work in performance.
   Contact with student work in other countries is consolidated
by frequent participation in student drama festivals in Europe,
and views are aired in the theatre magazine run from the Department by the students. "The play in performance" is kept
firmly in the centre of the academic discipline and given coher-
ence by a linking theme throughout the work of each session,
illustrating say, the emergence of the picture stage and similar
themes by appropriate production and associated study.
   The Drama Department in Manchester University was
founded in 1961—through the good offices of Granada Television Network, Ltd. Its aim is "to provide a liberal education
through a study of the theatre, in which emphasis is placed on
the practical application of the subject as well as on the contemporary crafts of the stage." The present Professor is Hugh
Hunt and there is a link with Bristol in that he was in 1946
the Bristol Old Vic's first Director of Productions. The degree
of B.A. Honours can concentrate either on the History of
Theatre, British and European, with practical work in acting,
costume, set design, lighting, etc. and playwriting, or on a
Joint Honours course of English, French or German and Drama.
In 1964, a postgraduate Diploma course was instituted for
directors, designers and writers. This concentrates on scenic
design, theatre architecture, dramatic criticism, and the use of
theatre in education. Acting is specifically excluded. There is
highly specialized and thorough work with the BBC Northern
Region in radio and TV drama, and a special studio with
closed circuit TV. The Department's present premises are
cramped, both for practical and academic study, but a new

University Theatre has been built in the rapidly growing University area housing a professional company also.

Birmingham's Department of Drama and Theatre Arts, established in the Arts Faculty in 1964, is operating under similarly difficult conditions in a studio and converted lecture theatre, but will eventually have a University Theatre. Under its director, John Russell Brown, who has spent a good deal of time in drama departments in the United States, drama can at present be studied mainly as one of the two subjects required for a Combined Subjects degree, a three-year course with Modern Languages, Greek or Latin, Music or Physical Education. This line introduces the student to all the arts involved in the performance of a play in a theatre. Drama may also be taken as a Supplementary subject, also over three years, or for two years as a Subsidiary.

Drama may also flourish under the aegis of the English Department, as in the University of Hull, where the study was inaugurated in 1963. It is there regarded as "a broad discipline within which to study the theatre as a social phenomenon and an autonomous means of artistic expression." An all-purpose auditorium is being planned, to hold about 550, and, specifically for the study of drama, a studio theatre to hold 200 only, designed by Peter Moro. In the meanwhile, the student dramatic activity is lively: they mount productions frequently and the Arts Festival is becoming a regular event.

The establishment of the study of drama and the building of suitable plant are proceeding also in the Universities of Sheffield and Exeter. The Northcott Theatre in Exeter serves the local community which has no other professional theatre. The sum of £100,000 was granted by a local millionaire for this express purpose: the University provided the site and underwrites the costs of maintenance and administration. The whole enterprise is closely linked with the University's Department of Music, and a very interesting Arts Centre project should emerge from this co-ordination of interests.

The Arts Centre as a complex of buildings to house in close juxtaposition the performing and visual arts is a familiar idea in the States, and the Johns Hopkins Centre at Dartmouth, New England, is only one of the many which spring to mind.

In Britain it is a comparatively new idea, and where better can it be practically expressed than in the many new universities which are being established?

Thus the University of Sussex, near Brighton, has a special grant from the Gulbenkian Foundation for a complex to house music, the visual arts, and a small theatre-workshop. The Director will have the status of a Senior Member, and artists-in-residence (also familiar figures of the American scene) will give their advice and guidance. Lancaster has already been mentioned, and there are indications that Warwick may follow suit. A theatre is being planned in the proposed Arts Centre in Warwick and Peter Hall, of the Royal Shakespeare Company, has been made an Associate Professor.

In the controversy about the status of drama in the Universities in the States, sparked off by Mr. W. McNeil Lowry of the Ford Foundation, much emphasis was laid on the professional standard, not always well served by the proliferation of drama in an academic world unless there is a strong connection with the professional theatre. British universities are increasingly taking the responsibility for professional companies as well as their student activities. Like Exeter, Southampton University has a new theatre, the Nuffield, so-called because its building was financed by the Nuffield Foundation, opened in 1960. As well as providing the *milieu* for student productions, it has a full and regular programme of visiting companies, for theatres, ballet, opera and related activities. There is no theatre in the town, and so it is in a sense a community theatre. It has no drama department and no courses in theatre arts.

Oxford has a variation on the same theme. The Playhouse, opened on its present site in 1938, has always been a repertory theatre with a resident professional company. It was acquired in 1961 by the University of Oxford and entitled the University Theatre, but the tradition of a resident company continues. The eight weeks of terms are shared equally between this company and college and university dramatic societies. Undergraduate activity is autonomous and there is no drama department or related academic courses.

There is considerable benefit to be gained on both sides from this fruitful working side by side of undergraduates and professionals, which will, one hopes, increase as the régime becomes

more established. Exeter, Manchester, Oxford and Southampton show the beginning of a pattern.

The administrative side of the theatre is comparatively
neglected in universities, except in the experience gained in
putting on plays either independently or under the guidance
of the mentors. Unless the teachers have actual theatre experience, and unless the students work within the disciplines
of a theatre run on professional lines, not self-governed by the
students themselves, administrative procedure is "picked up"
in a rather haphazard way.

It may be argued that this aspect of management is, like
acting, no proper concern of a university. It is, however,
fundamentally an essential for the proper display, through
correct and efficient channels, of all the artistic and literary
study that has gone into the play itself. Perhaps some of
the newer universities which are including Management Studies
in their curricula may be able to put this right. So much
accountancy, knowledge of the law, of professional and trades
unions, etc., are integral parts of the theatre manager's training.

Sir Tyrone Guthrie, whose work as Director of the theatre
named after him in Minneapolis has brought him into contact
with many Drama Departments in the Universities of the
United States, distinguishes between them as directed either
to the practical or the academic side of theatre, and propounds
interesting theories about the relation between them—

> I should have thought it reasonable that different univer-
> sities should have different aims for their Drama Depart-
> ments. Some will prefer to concentrate on theory and these
> will be staffed by scholars and teachers. Others might prefer
> to emphasize the practical side and come near to offering a
> trade-school training. In that case the faculty should have
> a high degree of practical competence and experience.[1]

If the study of drama in universities can develop in this
direction, it could balance the values of success and artistic
merit which are often confused in the professional theatre
because in the theatre as Guthrie adds—

> Few of us have time or energy to inquire seriously why we are
> doing what we are doing, or indeed, what we are really doing.

[1] *In Various Directions*, essay on *Theatre and the University* (Michael Joseph, 1965).

## Notes

Information from universities about qualifications in drama and related activities in the arts should be sought from the Registrar in each case. Details may also be found in the publication, *English: A Course Comparison Guide* (CRAC, Bateman Street, Cambridge).

Colleges of education which have drama as a main subject can be selected from the *Handbook of Colleges and Departments of Education* (Methuen, 1968). Information about departments of education which provide method courses for art graduates who wish to teach drama can be obtained from the Graduate Teacher Training Registry, 151 Gower Street, London, W.C.1.

Drama schools which include teacher training courses in their curriculum are listed for information by the Department of Education, F.6.2., Richmond Terrace, London, S.W.1.

# 6

## THE AMATEUR THEATRE

IT is a widely held belief that in the theatre as well as in ball games there is some special virtue in amateurism. As a result of this delusion the professional tends to adopt a self-defensive attitude of contemptuous antagonism towards the non-professional, who is equally often inclined to assume a self-complacent attitude of moral rectitude. Neither attitude is justifiable: both professional and amateur have the same basic purpose . . . the sale of entertainment to the public by the companies or the societies of which they are members.

The conflict is, in fact, declining. It is significant that wherever there is agitation for the establishment of a professional Civic Theatre there are usually several prominent non-professionals who are helping to lead the agitation. In many areas there is a close co-operation between the professionals and the amateurs in the sharing of whatever facilities are available for their performances. It seems certain that this co-operation will expand, with considerable benefit to both.

The amateur theatre in Britain is very varied. It has been estimated that there are something like 30,000 organizations regularly producing plays, musicals, opera, ballet, pantomime, etc. The quality of performance is also very varied. Most of them probably play once or twice each year in hired halls, theatres or cinemas, possibly for a week or perhaps for a few nights only. Their audiences may average a hundred or two per performance in a school or village hall but many of the large societies can fill theatres with capacities of a thousand or two.

Many amateur companies have their own theatres, either specially built or created from buildings that formerly functioned as churches, factories, warehouses and the like. One of the first theatres built in the UK after the 1939 war was the Middlesbrough Little Theatre with a seating capacity of 500 and costing £50,000, which was raised by the amateur company itself. The beginning of the Little Theatre movement is generally credited to the Stockport Garrick Society, founded in 1901, a movement that has since spread to all the English-speaking countries.

The growth of the amateur theatre has been quite remarkable. As the commercial theatres closed down all over the country, as a result of the competition of the cinema and later of television, the majority of the population were without any live theatres within reasonable distance of their homes. Quite understandably, the people proceeded to make their own theatre. The live theatre has been preserved in many areas by the amateurs, who have certainly helped to make possible the revival of professional theatre that is now evident. It seems probable that many community theatres will be built and will be used by professional and non-professional performers of all kinds. Numerous projects are under consideration and are in various stages of planning.

The difference between the theatres that are exclusively professional and those that may be partially or exclusively amateur is largely one of scale and detail. It is quite usual for the amateur dramatic and operatic societies to have members who are business executives, bank managers, accountants, solicitors and others who are professional in their own fields, men and women who, because of their interest in theatre are willing to devote most of their leisure time to the running of their societies or their theatres. It should not be necessary, therefore, to isolate the administration of the non-professional theatre, as these people are fully competent to extract from this survey such information and comment as may be usefully applied to their own activities.

For the benefit of the less-experienced members of amateur societies it should, perhaps, be stressed that, however large or small the organization may be, it should have a legal form of constitution. It will incur all kinds of liabilities through the activities of various individual members and it must be realized that all the members can be held jointly and severally responsible. The officials should make certain that their rules have been carefully examined by a solicitor. They can obtain detailed advice, if such be necessary, from their national bodies, the British Drama League, the National Operatic and Dramatic Association and the Little Theatres Guild.

## VARIOUS OBLIGATIONS

Amateurs are bound as strictly as professionals to keep the rules and the law in the following diverse matters (which are dealt with in fuller detail in Part II)—

1. The Performing Right Society's payments for copyrighted music.

2. The payment of royalties for all plays on which there is a copyright existing, according to the contract with the author, either direct or with his agent.

3. The payment of hire fees for orchestral scores and band parts.

4. Insurance of the physical assets of the production (set, costumes, properties, etc.), whether the society's own or on hire.

5. Insurance of the personnel. *Note.* All-inclusive policies covering All Rights for theatrical productions by amateurs are available for reasonable premiums from several insurance companies.

6. Any legal fees incurred in transactions with agents, theatres, etc.

7. The conditions of the Theatre Licence if they are using a public theatre (e.g. all their scenery must be fireproofed, nothing must be set downstage of the safety curtain, etc.).

8. The internal rules of the theatre, e.g. no visitors backstage during the performance, no actor in make-up or costumes to leave the theatre premises, etc.—all the normal rules which are usually pinned up in a prominent position backstage.

9. All conditions laid down by the fire authorities, the police, or other local bodies, either connected with the Theatre Licence or imposed independently, e.g. permission required for the use of naked lights and firearms, the employment of children, etc.

10. The conditions of the contract with the Theatre

management. This will stipulate in detail most of the production requirements in the same form as for contracts with professional companies. Indeed, amateurs would be wise to insist upon a recognized and detailed form of contract, rather that the vague letter of engagement which is sometimes offered "between friends," as it were, or a gentlemen's agreement. These can leave several matters too vague, and lead to recriminations later. When money is involved and a considerable knowledge of the way a theatre works is needed, it is best to have everything clearly set out before a final agreement is made. The society then knows more or less exactly what the obligations and requirements are, and can also allow in the preliminary estimates for expenses which the theatre may be taking for granted as the visitor's responsibility, but which can cause nasty shocks if not specifically stated in detail.

# 7

## THEATRE BUILDINGS

BECAUSE no manager operates in a vacuum, a word about theatre planning may not come amiss. It could be said bluntly and without flippancy that theatre-building is becoming all the rage. There is a slightly dangerous tendency to regard a theatre as a status symbol and a good way of meeting the cultural needs of a community whose material needs are already well looked after. The urge to build a theatre is basically a healthy and beneficial one, and more who propose to do so are now becoming increasingly sensible of the need to seek expert advice from those experienced in running theatres and from theatre consultants. They are also aware of the need to engage the manager of a new theatre for a long enough period of time before its opening for him to take part in the planning of the building. The planning and administration are indissoluble both in the physical aspect of the building and its financial framework. This chapter is not intended to be an exhaustive examination of everything that goes into the project of a new theatre building, but to summarize a few basic principles which all concerned should bear in mind and to raise some of the questions which must be answered before the project gets to the drawing board or to the astute Finance Committee of a local authority or of the Arts Council.

### THE LOCAL AUDIENCE

No two theatres are exactly comparable nor is it possible to transplant an exact copy of a flourishing theatre to a locality which is quite different. It should not be possible for a minority group to impose a theatre on a community without sounding out as many opinions as possible. If, for instance, there has already been a theatre in the area, why did it fail? Was the standard of performance too low? Was the building unprepossessing? Was the failure caused by bad management, bad publicity, failure to gauge the taste of the audience, a badly planned programme of attractions? If no theatre has ever existed there, is this due to lack of demand? Has there ever been any indication that if a theatre were supplied it would attract an audience?

How far away is the nearest flourishing theatre and how many people take trips to it from the town for which the new one is proposed? Have the local amateur societies premises adequate for their needs or would they be interested in taking their built-in audiences with them to a new theatre? Has the local education authority an interest in following the modern trend in regarding the theatre as a fruitful pursuit for their pupils?

Provided that these subjective factors are found to be as promising as it is possible to gauge theoretically, the next stage may be examined. If the omens so far point to the building of a theatre, the really essential question to be posed is— What is its purpose and the scope of its proposed activity?

### THE POSSIBLE SCOPE OF THE THEATRE'S ACTIVITY

The kind of building needed, the cost of running it and the kind of administration needed all depend on the crystallizing of its aims. This process needs an early and thorough statistical and sociological survey of the town and the region in which the theatre is to be situated.

Theatrical competitors in the nearest larger towns must be taken into account. If there is already one of the large regional touring theatres which can economically afford and physically accommodate the National Theatre, Royal Shakespeare, Covent Garden and other touring companies, then obviously it is not feasible to plan a similar operation.

In a sparsely populated region, devoid of theatre or indeed of any centre or cultural activity, it may be worth considering the cost of a building which can take large-scale tours and of one which can supply also the need for music and art. Even so, it must be borne in mind that one visit per annum from all the famous national companies would not make a season, and that maintaining anything like a coherent programme in a large building would be difficult and financially hazardous.

Another factor is the seasonal one. Some towns enjoy a tourist season and might do well by providing good productions during these peak periods. The off-peak periods might serve for the local activity. In this case a smaller and less expensively-run theatre would be suitable.

### FINANCE

Expert theatre consultants and architects can supply estimates for a building once the brief is established, and no generalization can be made on this point. What must be emphasized is that the building of the theatre is only the beginning of the problem. Side by side with the spatial plans there must be the costing of the administration of the building in terms of staff needed, heating, lighting, supplies, recurrent and non-recurrent, as well as the rates and rent. These items are on the outgoing side and it is equally important to make as good a guess as possible on the income side in terms of size of auditorium, ticket prices and audience percentage. These can perhaps be only notional in the very early stages, but it is no use providing a building which cannot be serviced properly, whether by agreed subsidy forthcoming over a long period or by box-office receipts and rents from users, or, as is more usual, by a combination of both. A policy-planning body should work from the beginning with the premises-planning body. That is why the initial basic decision on the purpose and scope of the theatre's use must be clearly laid down.

### GENERAL PLANNING PRINCIPLES

The economy of the building and its easy running depend greatly on logical planning and relation of the various "cells" of activity.

The stage area and equipment are not included in these observations which concern primarily the organization of the theatre.

## 1. *Audience Facilities*

A self-evident principle to follow in the planning of audience
facilities is that circulation should be followed through in terms
of what any theatre-goer normally needs.  For instance, take
a Mr. and Mrs. A. and their child (under 18) and plot their
programme—

On arrival, they may need to collect their tickets for the performance from the Box Office.  Ergo, the Box Office must be
near the entrance, not too far from the auditorium either if
they have cut it fine and have to go straight in.  They should
not be hindered by a queue waiting to book for other performances, so the Box Office must have a window for "This
Performance Only."  They should not have to push past other
people waiting for their friends and the foyer should be so
planned that early arrivals are not in the fairway and can sit
or stand there without being jostled.

The family safely armed with tickets may then wish to leave
their coats and shopping and indeed, following the Continental example, should be encouraged to do so.  The cloakrooms
must be of adequate size and in the same complex as the Box
Office.  So with the lavatories; the Ladies' and Gentlemen's
lavatories should not be too widely separate from each other.
Whether or not there are lavatories elsewhere, there must be
some sited very near the foyer, where everything must facilitate
easy and quick access to the auditorium or hasty exit from it
(essential when schools performances are held in the theatre!).

If Mr. and Mrs. A. have arrived early, they may wish to
have a drink.  They must be able to reach the bar easily, be
served quickly and reach the auditorium without going back
on their tracks too often or meeting a flow towards the auditorium moving in the opposite direction.  Their child is not
allowed in licensed premises, so they should be able to buy an
orange-squash or ice-cream for him from a separate but adjacent
counter, so that he is not frighteningly separated from them.

Access to the auditorium should be planned to avoid contrary
movements or crossing of streams of people.  There should
be entrances leading easily to the foyer, bars, restaurant, etc.,
to allow people who are approaching from these directions
to get in easily and quickly—especially important for punctual

reassembly after an interval. Fire regulations come into the planning of these entrances too, remember. If steps can be eliminated or ramps added here and there, it is very helpful for the elderly and the disabled. Some provision can always usefully be made for the storage of wheel chairs.

Having planned your circulation, signpost it clearly! Make sure that the signs are above head-level, with divided access for special seat-numbers particularly clearly shown. If smoking is not allowed in the auditorium, make this known in the foyer, so that the unwitting offender who gets by with a cigarette is spared the embarrassment of smothering it where no ash-trays are provided.

Make sure that there is a landing or obvious point of vantage where the House Manager may stand and be clearly seen, preferably near the Box Office where ticket queries or other questions need to be sorted out.

## 2. *Grouped Activities*

It is obvious that staff whose work is related should have office space in the same area, but this, alas, does not always seem to happen in practice. The administrative staff should be given offices far enough away from the public and the audience to give them privacy for work yet near enough to be on call. This applies particularly to the Administrator, who should have an office to himself with his secretary in a second office to guard the door against the stream of callers. Her office could well have a sliding door, open for communicaton, closed for interviews or telephone calls.

The House Manager should be nearer the scene of action, especially when he is required to be on duty during performances. It is no bad thing to have him near the Box Office.

The Catering area is another "cell" in the theatre, with the Catering Manager near enough to be aware what is happening but able to do bookwork in peace. The placing of kitchen and service areas in relation to the bars and restaurants is an exercise needing specialized planning and the whole has to be carefully sited *vis-à-vis* the auditorium for circulation purposes. If it can also serve a staff canteen backstage so much the better, with kitchen and storage areas midway between front of house and backstage.

SPECIAL FACILITIES

According to its basic purpose and potential users, some special facilities may be needed. These apply mainly to stage and technical requirements, but are noted here, as they cannot easily be added to an existing building.

*For Touring Companies*

A large scene dock for companies bringing more than one production and more storage and wing space are needed than for an average resident company. Naturally if the site is large enough the more space which can be allocated to any stage area the better, but this ideal state of affairs is rare.

An office back-stage addition to that of the resident stage manager is also desirable.

Parking space for the large specially-designed lorries used by many touring companies is needed, adjacent to the theatre if possible, whereas the normal delivery of stage supplies and scenery for a small repertory theatre might not call for such permanent provision.

*For a Repertory Company*

An adequate rehearsal room is desirable in any theatre, but is essential for a producing company permanently using a theatre.

Permanent companies also build up great quantities of valuable assets in the shape of scenery, furniture and costumes. They need a good workshop for handling scenery, space for making properties, spraying costumes, etc., a work-room for making costumes and, of course, increasing space to store all these assets. A theatre catering mainly for touring and amateur companies might not need to cater so fully for these needs.

*For Opera and Music*

If the theatre is to be used for opera, ballet, recitals and concerts as well as plays, provision must be made from the beginning for special facilities. An orchestra pit, whether permanent or on a hydraulic system to make it serve as forestage or part of the auditorium seating, must be planned for the maximum

number which need to be adequately seated. There must be
a band-room for the orchestra, and provision for their hats
and coats and instrument cases. The equipment for concerts
and recitals might have to include rostra for choirs, an acoustic
shell for smaller ensembles, a number of chairs used exclusively
for choirs and orchestras and not illicitly filched from some
other part of the building.

### For Related Activities

If the theatre is to be a centre for several community activities, such as gramophone societies, meetings of local groups
needing to use films or slides, committee meetings, receptions,
it is as well to allocate specially designed space for them. If
smaller rooms, which can be used independently of the main
part of the theatre and auditorium can be included in the plan,
it is economical in the end to do so. Their heating and lighting
should be independent of the main building, and access to these
rooms should similarly not involve using the main foyer. They
can then be used either when the theatre is closed without
needing to put the main systems into operation, or when the
theatre is in use without colliding with its main activities. A
proper time-table can be arranged without any fear that the
room may be sucked into use for an emergency rehearsal, for
instance, at the last moment.

There are dangers in thinking that a large part of the theatre
can serve many disparate purposes. That way madness and
confusion lie, as well as unnecessary expense and wear and
tear.

These observations could be multiplied and the space
relationships are indeed better indicated in diagram form. This
has been done very clearly in the publications by the Association
of British Theatre Technicians, Theatre Planning One and
Two, together with much valuable comment and useful statistics. The theatre perfect for all its purposes from the beginning
has yet to be built, but the intelligent application of general
principles and working out therefore of a minutely detailed
brief can avoid many of the pitfalls.

# 8

# TRAINING OF THEATRE
# PERSONNEL

IT would be unthinkable to aspire to entry to many professions without recognizing the need for a stringent preliminary training, and the theatre is now no exception. I say "now," because for many years it was thought, and indeed was perhaps the case in practice, that a short cut to acquiring the necessary skills was to join a repertory theatre in a humble capacity and pick up knowledge as one went along. There is some truth in the central fact here, that purely theoretical knowledge is useless unless it is applied to the job in hand, but the basic truth cannot be too often recalled that theatre is finally a business. It is moreover a world in which competition is fierce and there are always too many people chasing too few jobs. Finally, and most important, large sums of money are involved, whether from private sources, charitable trusts, the Arts Council subsidies or local authorities, and the market for theatre is one which has to be fought for every inch of the way and every day of the year. No theatre, whether commercial or subsidized, can now afford to carry passengers, or to spend any of its cash on learners who are not specifically given the status of trainees with all the teaching and supervision that this status implies.

For anyone wishing to enter the profession in any department it may be useful to categorize some of the best channels of entry. Account has been taken in a separate chapter of the courses available in universities, so the references given here exclude university training. No attempt is made to give details of the actual courses available. These change from time to time, and the latest current information should be sought direct from the source.

## ADMINISTRATION

This was until recent years the post for which specific training was almost entirely lacking except within the theatre
itself, but the recognition of the need for trained managers has
now led to the careful consideration of how the training may
be formally acquired.

### 1. *Trainee Administrator's Scheme Run by the Arts Council of Great Britain*

The source of information is the Drama Department, Arts
Council of Great Britain, 105 Piccadilly, London, WIV OAU.

The process of application begins with a letter to the appropriate officer, the Assistant Drama Director, briefly stating
enough qualifications to serve as a starting point. This is
usually followed by an interview with an officer of the Drama
Department. The most likely applicants then go forward for
a further interview with a small committee, composed of the
Arts Council Officer and theatre managers from a selection of
theatres of various kinds, some representing the Council of
Repertory Theatres, others currently serving on the Arts
Council Drama Panel, or thought to be suitably qualified for
other reasons. The length of the course is flexible according
to the experience and qualifications of the applicant. The
longest period is one year, but there are six-month courses
and sometimes even shorter ones, for, say, someone who has
already had experience of some kind in theatres and who
wishes to broaden his outlook, or study a particular activity.
Whatever the length of the course, the practice is common to
all. Trainees are sent to several theatres of different kinds for
varying lengths of time. The managers of these theatres undertake the responsibility of allowing the trainee to participate as
fully as possible in all the activities of the theatre, spending
time backstage if this seems advisable, as well as with the management. The outstanding value of this scheme is that it takes
place in working theatres. Participation in all kinds of work
often enables the trainee to discover special aptitudes and he
may, one hopes, compare and evaluate ideas which he can
later develop when he has a post of his own.

2. *The Polytechnic School of Management Studies, London, W.*1
*The Administration of the Arts* (course arranged in conjunction
with the Arts Council of Great Britain). This scheme came
into being in 1967. It aims to impart the essential technical,
legal and management information and techniques, and to
combine a lecture course with practical work in periods spent
in theatres. Its lecturers include theatre people as well as those
more strictly trained in the technique of management studies.
It is at the time of writing too early to report on its results, as
the first batch of students have only just completed the course,
but it should prove an immensely valuable way of increasing
the numbers of trained administrators needed for the arts.
Here again, as for the Arts Council scheme, the numbers are
comparatively limited, and initial interviewing for the number
selected is done in association with the Arts Council.

3. *Trainee Management in Theatres*
There are some theatres, Sadler's Wells Theatre and the
Oxford Playhouse, for instance, which have their own trainee
scheme. Young people who wish to learn theatre management
are taken on to the strength at a modest salary and work as
part of the theatre staff. They may be assigned to the administrator, with special duties of their own—publicity, front-of-
house duties, etc.—but are sent also into all the other departments to study and absorb the methods particular to each area.
This kind of traineeship may be particularly valuable to young
people who have already spent some years at a university,
where they may have had a good deal of experience of theatre,
whether independently or in a Drama Department. It works
very well also for those of mature years who may already have
a training they can apply to theatre, e.g. in public relations,
in education, or in the catering which is becoming an increasingly important asset to the theatre facilities.

ACTING AND STAGE MANAGEMENT

(i) *Drama Academies.* This highly specialized training is best
undertaken in a drama academy. These training establishments are the natural nurseries for young theatre personnel

and the theatres have a responsibility towards their products. While there is as yet no rule of "controlled entry" into the profession, i.e. the employment of those only who have been through an accepted form of training, there is in general a bias towards those who thus qualified, which is right and proper.

Once the course is completed, the student is in the jungle of competition. Managements from the West End and from provincial theatres make a point of attending the end-of-term productions which provide the shop-window for the students and some fortunate ones may be snapped up at once. For many others the dreary routine of writing round to managements (with photographs and a *curriculum vitae*,) and of badgering agents, has then to begin.

A useful list of drama schools can be found in *Contacts*, the hand-book of theatre information issued by Spotlight Casting Directory and obtainable from: Spotlight Limited, 43 Cranbourn Street, London, W.C.2. It is published twice a year.

(ii) *Student Contracts.* There is a very small intake of young people into repertory by means of the Student Contract, which is approved by the Provincial Theatre Council and which has to be countersigned in each case by this body. It applies to repertory companies only, and the number of students taken on this basis is dictated by the size of the regular company, i.e. when there are eight artists or fewer, not more than two students may be employed; with more than eight artists, the number of students may not exceed more than twenty per cent of the total permanent company (including the students). The numbers are also regulated by the length of the season, and there must be an initial trial period of rehearsal and one production. These and other observations and rules are set out in the contract itself, copies of which can be obtained from British Actors' Equity Association, 8 Harley Street, London, W.1.

### DIRECTORS AND DESIGNERS

There is, alas, no way of neatly categorizing the channels through which these may emerge, mainly because the number of them who can consistently find employment is small and only the gifted can finally survive. A fortunate few can be taken as assistant directors, often straight from university, by companies such as the National Theatre, Royal Shakespeare and Royal Court. This experience of working with the most highly experienced directors in a permanent company is, of course, invaluable, but is restricted to a very small number. They then often proceed to become resident artistic directors of smaller companies.

Help from the Arts Council may be forthcoming in various ways for would-be directors and designers, and established ones may, if they have a special case, acquire a modest bursary to study chosen aspects of the theatre in other countries. The special conditions in which application may be made for these benefits by an aspiring or established director or designer come under review from time to time. The relevant information should be sought from the Arts Council when needed so that it is up to date.

The BBC and other television companies have schemes for general traineeships, which include the aim of grooming directors and designers. These are competitive and, as for the Arts Council scheme, details of the conditions of entry vary and must be obtained from the source.

While there are these organized schemes with financial help, directors and designers often emerge, of course, from within the theatre. Both need individual creative talent which may occur in an individual of any kind of background or formal training. These gifts often become apparent in the Universities because of the proliferation there of organized or independent dramatic activity. Events such as the National Union of Students National Student Drama Festival, sponsored by a national newspaper, give great publicity to student drama. The entries for this competitive festival are adjudicated by professional theatre people and reach a very high standard of presentation. A commercial management has this year further extended the possibilities by offering a money prize to the author of the best play entered for the Festival and to the student body which presents it. This may well prove a strong incentive to new writing talent and certainly to the young director who has to put a new play through its paces with student actors.

ust as directors may emerge through the Universities, or even through notable and flourishing amateur dramatic societies, designers may come through drama academies, some of which have specially good design departments, and through art schools.

## Technical Staff

The Council of Repertory Theatres and the Association of British Theatre Technicians are evolving training schemes for stage staff, to be worked out in theatres as distinct from training establishments. The number of trainees is strictly limited and the details of the training schemes are in process of completion.

### TRAINING FOR DRAMA IN EDUCATION

The achievement of the teachers' training colleges which offer drama as a subject, Principal or Subsidiary, is much underrated. Many of them, through a University Department of education or under a local authority, give special diplomas for drama, or may link it with related subjects. The range of study is wide, and students usually work in close collaboration with other departments and use all the resources which other techniques can offer them for practical use. Where a farsighted theatre exists in the same area there is often a lively connection and the students are keen and critical theatregoers.

## General note on Training

In the spring of 1969 the Arts Council set up a special committee to examine and report on the various facilities for theatre training in all its aspects. The report and recommendations of this committee will give a full picture of what is being done and of what may be done in the future.

# 9

## RECRUITMENT OF THEATRE PERSONNEL

THERE are some recognized methods of engaging theatre personnel after their training, which may be helpful in outline.

### ACTORS

#### I. SPOTLIGHT
The focal point of reference for actors and managers seeking each other out is the magnificently organized Spotlight Casting Agency. This has various aspects—

#### (i) *Photo-directories*
It issues large volumes of photographs of actors and actresses, also children, which give details helpful to casting, such as notes of previous experience, height, colouring, etc., and the name of the agent to whom application about availability should be made. Those who wish to be included pay for advertisement. Managements also are listed, together with theatres, London and provincial, who pay for space and who in return receive copies of the photo-directories. A director casting a play riffles endlessly through the pages looking for the actor who catches his fancy as suitable for the parts he has in mind. The process then begins of ringing the agents to discuss dates and terms and to arrange for an interview. "Spotlight" often helps in this respect and can supply telephone numbers of actors without agents, for instance.

#### (ii) *Interview Service*
Theatre directors from the provinces who have no office or club in town may wish to see a number of actors in London in

the space of a day rather than summon them to some far-flung outpost of theatre at the expense of time and money. "Spotlight" will provide the room in which the interviews may take place.

### (iii) *General Services*

The staff are extremely knowledgeable about the theatre world and can often supply the answers to all kinds of general queries with efficiency and helpfulness.

### 2. AGENTS

Nowadays the actor's agent is much more than his means of finding out what work is available—the agent is also his guide, philosopher and friend, ideally on a very personal basis. The first thing any young actor should do is to find an agent who is willing to put him "on the books." This implies that the agent recognizes and understands the actor's range and potentialities, that he will immediately inform the actor of casting going on for which he may be considered and that he will actively draw the attention of managers and directors to his client. When the actor lands the job, the agent's work of soliciting notice continues, to induce as many useful and influential people as possible to see his performance so that one job may lead to another. There is much more to the relationship than this, of course, and many actors struggling for a beginning in the theatre owe a lot to their agents in the form of practical help and encouragement in the lean times. This is not always, let me hasten to add, in the form of financial benefit, but in the expressed faith which combats the frightening loss of confidence and ensuing apathy which is the actor's greatest enemy in spells of unemployment.

There can also be a relationship of help and confidence between the agent and theatre directors and managers. A director may ask the agents in whom he trusts for suggestions about casting.

Negotiations about money must be carefully conducted on both sides (especially on the telephone, remembering the rule of verbal contract). Tentative suggestions should be followed up as soon as possible by written agreement and the exchange of the relevant standard contracts.

## STAGE-MANAGEMENT (INCLUDING DESIGNERS)

The recruitment of stage-staff is more difficult to define. They have no centrally organized agency which operates to the wide extent of the "Spotlight" service for actors, though many highly-qualified and experienced staff are included in that service. There are only a few other means of recruitment.

### 1. *Advertisement*

Theatres frequently advertise in the weekly newspaper of the profession—*Stage*. For key personnel the theatre may take quite large and prominent advertising space, giving details about the requirements of the post and sometimes an indication of the salary offered. There is also the column of Staff Wanted. Staff who are free can similarly take advertising space, either large or small insertions, with the knowledge that the paper is widely used for the purpose of finding staff.

### 2. *West End Stage-Management Association*

This body does its best to keep *au fait* with the availability and whereabouts of stage-management. It will supply information on request both to those of its members who are seeking work and to managements who are looking for personnel of the calibre which membership of this body suggests. The address at the time of writing is: 81 St. Mary's Grove, London, W.4.

The theatre is very much a world of personal contacts and allowance must be made for the grapevine in any account of sources of employment. In work which needs the building-up of a team, particularly in stage-management, there are many directors who prefer to keep the team together as much as possible. Most directors build up a "pool" of actors with whom they enjoy working and they keep the same stage-staff when they move to other theatres or, if free-lance, suggest to the management that they should employ staff already known to them. This is a very human process and one which can make for the creation of a special style and method. The director–designer team can be a particularly good relationship.

*General Note*

Any manager engaging staff unknown to him should, as in any profession, go carefully into the matter of references and qualifications. The written contract of employment must be according to recognized regulations of the relevant unions— e.g. NATKE, Equity—and any special conditions of work must be clearly stated before the contract is made. Slightly different qualifications may be needed according to the scope of the work, and it is too late for both parties to the contract if this information is not given. No printed standard form of contract, except for actors, can provide for all possible variations, and these must be settled from the beginning to the satisfaction of both parties.

# 10

# RELATED ARTS IN
# THE THEATRE

WITH the growth in popularity of the arts centre idea, where provision is made for many activities, the management must be conversant with many procedures. Even in a repertory theatre there is now quite a demand for the occasional talk, recital of verse and music, concert, reading, etc., and new buildings often have provision for films. The visual arts also have their place either in a separate room or on the walls of a bar or corridor. Everything that can be done to include these activities adds extra dimensions of interest but they need care and provision by the management. So a few notes of general guidance are given below.

## EXHIBITIONS

It is assumed that the exhibition will usually be of the work of one local artist or of a local group in the area served by the theatre. The exhibition of larger scope illustrating the career of a world-famous painter, or perhaps a theme, such as portraiture or Cubism, is normally beyond a theatre's scope, needing a preparatory period of years in some cases, special conditions and great expense.

For our more modest purpose, it can be assumed that the collecting of the paintings and arrangements for their transport to the theatre are the first problem, worked out between the artist and the theatre. If the theatre is doing the artist a service by giving his work a showing, much of the cost of transport, etc., may be borne by the artist. The framing costs are certainly the artist's concern. The theatre may, on the other hand, undertake the cost of transport in the hope of recouping all or part of these from an agreed percentage on sales. The important point is that a clear understanding on these points should be reached early in the arrangements. A friendly and vague agreement may lay up a great deal of future trouble. The artist must also be happy about the space allotted, the wall-surface against which the work will be hung, and the lighting.

The actual hanging of the exhibition is one calling for some knowledge of the way to relate pictures to each other in the happiest way, and the artist can be very helpful in these matters.

The catalogue can be compiled in either of two ways. It can be related to the exhibition after the hanging is completed, so that the numbering of the pictures is consecutive, helpful for reference as people move from one picture to another without having to search through their catalogues. The artist may prefer to have the work listed in another way, regardless of the hanging order, perhaps chronologically or by subject matter. The decision finally lies with the artist.

Insurance and security are the responsibility of the theatre. It is usual to take out "wall-to-wall" insurance, i.e. cover for the pictures from the time they leave the owner's possession till they are returned there. Supervision may present a problem when the exhibition is in a bar or other area of the theatre not used during the day, but open to access, and it adds to the costs. If the artist agrees to exhibit in these conditions without a supervisor, the insurance company must be informed of this fact, since it will affect the premium payable. It is also helpful for the insurance company if an annual premium is paid, covering all exhibitions, instead of making a piecemeal arrangement for each one separately. They will of course set a ceiling on the value of any one picture and must be informed if this is likely to be exceeded on any occasion.

A private view is pleasant for the artist and creates a potential special public for the exhibitions. If it can be arranged without interfering with the normal work of the theatre, it is more generous for the theatre to bear its costs unless the artist is particularly anxious to do so.

In return for these services, the theatre can legitimately ask for a percentage on sales. Anything up to, say, one-third is fair, and any money so gained goes to defraying the cost of printing, advertising, or other charges mentioned above. It may happen that by and large the exhibition expenses and income balance out, but a figure for them should be included

in the general budget. The enterprise is not greatly profit-
making in cash but is an amenity much appreciated by the
artists and by the theatre-public.

### 3. CONCERTS AND RECITALS

If the theatre holds a licence for Music, Singing and Dancing
and for Sunday performances of this nature, concerts and recitals are a valuable asset to its programme. There are many
one-man shows now available, and programmes of verse and
music are provided by several ensembles, often with very well-
known performers; these are all popular.

The easiest way is of course to engage them as a package
deal through an accredited agent. This avoids the complicated processes of arranging rehearsals, paying separate
copyright fees and entering into Musicians' Union contracts, all
of which must be carefully looked into if the entertainment is
promoted independently by the theatre.

Practical arrangements for these performances are sometimes rather *ad hoc*, lying as they do a little outside the normal
theatre routine. Care must be taken to provide efficient music-
stands, for instance, not those which collapse at a touch. The
chairs for players of musical instruments must be without arms
and of the correct height. Remember that the cello and double
bass are instruments which can slide away from the player
and his chair over a highly polished floor if both are not
islanded on a rug! Readers may need a solid yet elegant
lectern for their scripts with a special light carefully placed
so as not to dazzle the audience. If the reading is less formal,
comfortable chairs of a reasonable height are needed—it is no
use expecting the reader to have his legs higher than his head
in a reclining arm-chair. Proper allowance of time must be
made for rehearsals, especially for musicians, whose rehearsal
time and payment are strictly laid down by the Musicians'
Union and whose time must not be wasted.

Some attempt must be made to make the stage look attractive, but do not do this with banks of flowers without gentle
inquiry as to whether any of the performers is a hay-fever
sufferer! Many are the flower-arrangements which have been
jettisoned at the last moment for this surprisingly common reason.

LECTURES AND CONFERENCES

These would seem to be extremely simple to mount but there are one or two pitfalls which can be avoided by planning and forethought, to the greater happiness of all concerned. The lecturer should be asked beforehand whether he prefers a reading-desk or a table, and of what height. Assuming that he will have notes or a script, whether or not he reads from them, an adequate light for the desk must be provided. There is nothing more frustrating for a speaker than to find himself unable to read a quotation because of the subdued light in which his audience is happily sitting. An Anglepoise lamp or a tubular striplight fixed to the desk and turned away from the audience serves the purpose very well.

Some speakers like to have a microphone, especially if they are daunted by a large auditorium. They must then indicate whether they prefer a throat-microphone, one on the table or one on a separate stand. The electrician should test it with the speaker before the talk and should adjust it for height and volume. It is a reasonable precaution to have him standing by throughout, since faults all too easily develop without apparent reason.

If slides are to be used, the speaker must be asked well in advance to supply details of their size. If they are not of the normal standard sizes (and some Continental slides vary) a special slide-carrier must be procured and this cannot be done at the last minute. The slide-operator and the speaker should have a preliminary confabulation about signals for changing the slides and also check that the slides are in the correct order and the right way up. It is agony for all when the darkness is filled with muttered imprecations from the speaker or pictures appear upside down, and this ordeal can be averted by preparation.

FILMS

Even in these days of non-flam film, the use of cinema equipment in theatres is very carefully and strictly regulated by the local authority. Any theatre contemplating the use of films must make sure that the proposed projection-box is properly sited in the theatre and the equipment of a kind to comply with these regulations. No generalized summary of these protective measures would be widely useful, as the local police and fire authorities' rulings vary somewhat from place to place.

Provided that the showing of films is permitted and licensed, the first and obvious thing is to make sure that the operator is properly qualified—not all theatre electricians to whom this task may fall are qualified to use projectors without special training.

It is not too difficult to obtain films of special interest through organizations such as the British Film Institute as well as the normal distributors. For the sake of good relations with the cinemas in the area, it is as well for the theatre to plan its programmes with reference to those planned for the regular circuits, and to work in co-operation with the local cinemas rather than in competition. There are an increasing number of theatres, the Arts Theatre, Cambridge, for instance, and the Northcott Theatre in Exeter, which include films as a regular feature of their annual programme. They can also be a useful stand-by for gaps in the programme of theatres which have touring companies as their main attraction. Films, however, are in the main a subsidiary interest in theatres, hence the need for harmonious relations with cinemas proper.

The other item of equipment needed besides the projector is the screen. It is a great advantage if this can be incorporated in the proscenium opening, easily let down and concealed in a box permanently *in situ* when not in use. It should be of a kind which serves also for slide-projection for lectures, and advice about the surface and texture can be obtained from specialist suppliers of such equipment.

The importance of forward planning must be stressed. Films are very popular, especially the 16-millimetre suitable for small screens and for educational purposes, so bookings must be made with the distributors as far ahead as possible.

**II**

# THE ARTS COUNCIL OF
# GREAT BRITAIN

THE Arts Council of Great Britain, from which many blessings
flow, distributes to the arts, through the Department of Education and Science, the amount of Government money allotted
for this purpose.  At some time a definitive history of its origins
and development will surely be written and here only the brief-
est outlines, which can hardly do justice to its 28-year-long
career, can be indicated.

Its origin was in the bleak war years, improvised in 1939
to keep the arts alive and to bring them to the displaced and
deprived communities of Great Britain.  In this form it was
the Committee for the Encouragement of Music and the Arts
(affectionately known as CEMA) and was given a send-off
with £25,000 from the Pilgrim Trust and a further £25,000
from the Government.  In 1940 it was sponsored by the Ministry of Education and voted a grant-in-aid from the Exchequer.
Landmarks in its history are the Chairmanship of Lord Keynes
in 1942; the setting-up of advisory Panels of specialists in the
arts of the theatre, music, art and literature; its incorporation
with Charter in 1954; in the next year the decision to allot
its income direct from the Treasury.  Finally in 1965 its responsibility was transferred to the Department of Education
and Science whose Under-Secretary, Miss Jennie Lee, became
Minister with special responsibility for the arts.

In 1966 a new Royal Charter of Incorporation was granted,
and the aim of the Council's work was reiterated thus—"to
develop and improve the knowledge, understanding and
practice of the arts . . . . to increase the accessibility of the
arts to the public throughout Great Britain."

The work has developed from the sending out of individual
artists and tours of plays, opera and ballet to war-darkened
Britain to the disposal of £5,700,000 in 1966–7, taking less part

in the direct promotion and management of such enterprises. It concentrates on the consolidation of proven theatres and companies and the encouragement of those which seem to fill a gap in the artistic picture or intend to serve an area hitherto barren of the arts. It is also directed by the terms of the Charter to work with other bodies concerned directly or indirectly with the arts, whether local authorities or Government departments, and to act as a "partner in patronage." It does not aim to dictate policy or improve taste. Under the New Royal Charter the measure of autonomy enjoyed by the former Scottish and Welsh Committees of the Arts Council was signified by their new titles—the Scottish Arts Council and the Welsh Arts Council. So the patterns of the arts particular to these regions have particular decentralized attention.

The main headings of Arts Council activity may be summarized briefly as follows.

### DRAMA

#### 1. *Allocation of Subsidy*

Grants are allocated to theatres and allied projects in proportion as far as possible to their current needs and further plans, on the evidence of artistic and financial achievement and with the support of detailed balance sheets and estimates of future income and expenditure. Major subsidies go to the national companies—the Royal Opera House, Covent Garden, the Royal Shakespeare Company and Sadler's Wells. Considerable sums go to the theatres categorized as "in association with the Arts Council of Great Britain," the established regional repertory theatres—Bristol, Nottingham, Coventry, Birmingham, Oxford, Liverpool and Sheffield—and proportionately smaller ones to other theatres in the province. These grants are, with box-office receipts, the mainstay of operating costs, and are allocated through the Drama Department.

#### 2. *Capital Expenditure*

The Council has a special allocation for capital expenditure for the building of new theatres and also for the purchase of equipment, improvements and extensions of buildings, etc.,

for which application may be made when the need arises for
equipment or a project too costly to be met out of the theatre's
normal running budget.

### 3. *Touring Grants and Guarantees*

For companies which tour either full-time (such as Prospect
Productions and the Ballet Rambert) or regularly for part of
the year, grants and guarantees against loss on the costs of
these operations are allocated, provided that equitable contracts are agreed with the host theatres, so that the possible
loss is not borne entirely by the visiting company, thus dis-
sipating the grant given for work in its home base.

### 4. *New Drama and Neglected Plays*

The range of plays presented by regional theatres has become
very wide. The encouragement of new playwrights and of
managements who are willing to take a risk on new plays is
furthered by the offer of special guarantees against loss incurred in such productions. Audiences are naturally more
wary of an unknown play, either by a new author or in translation, and even if attendance builds up after a slow start,
low receipts at the beginning of the run cannot always be com-
pensated for by tardily full houses towards the end.

Similarly, many classics are worthy of inclusion in an imaginative programme, but have for various reasons dropped out
of the usual or fashionable repertoire. Several Jacobean and
eighteenth-century plays have, for instance, been given a new
showing by reason of a special guarantee against loss under
the heading of "neglected plays."

### 5. *Transport Subsidies*

This scheme is intended to build a regular audience by encouraging party bookings, and is a great boon particularly to
theatres which serve a wide rural area as well as their own
home town. The theatre management must apply to the
Council for participation in this scheme. It is operated in
various ways according to local idiosyncrasies, but the gist of
the benefit is a two-fold one. The theatre gains by building
up a regular section of party-bookings and potential patrons
living at a distance have a reduced transport cost and tickets

offered by the theatre at a reduced party rate. On each fare over a certain sum, at present 1s. 6d., one-third is refunded. The refund is not to exceed a maximum of two-thirds of the amount paid for tickets. The theatre pays the reduction due so that visiting parties get prompt refunds, and submits a claim to the Arts Council later, making the process as easy and encouraging as possible.

### 6. *Help to Other Theatre Projects*

In addition to direct aid to theatres and their projects, sums of money of a lesser magnitude are given from time to time to organizations which benefit the theatre in general, e.g. to the periodical *Gambit,* which publishes little-known plays, to the Association of British Theatre Technicians, the British Centre of the International Theatre Institute, to name only a few.

### MUSIC

Opera, ballet, orchestras, festivals of music and vocal, choral and instrumental ensembles come under this section of the Council and money is allocated through the Music Department.

### ART

Exhibitions of importance and wide range are regularly mounted for London galleries and for special occasions elsewhere. Others are designed especially for touring, particularly to places which have no large art gallery of their own. Art clubs and some small but distinguished galleries in the provinces also receive help.

### LITERATURE

Attention is paid by this department to both the spoken and the written word (excluding drama, of course). Organizations which present programmes including verse, festivals of literature and some periodicals presenting collections of contemporary verse are all included.

## ARTS CENTRES AND ARTS ASSOCIATIONS

An increasingly large category for the allocation of Arts Council money includes the confederation of interests which promotes the arts regionally. Some are very large, such as the North-Eastern Association of the Arts, covering a wide area and with an elaborate programme, others purely local, perhaps only a small but valuable group in one town. It is to these growing concerns which link local authorities and local industry in a concerted effort to promote the arts that particular attention will undoubtedly be given in the future. They can provide a variety of entertainment, exhibitions and the like in a pro-grammed whole, not in the more wasteful and diffuse manner which is all that individual efforts by theatres or small groups can provide. They can also help to create a pattern of develop-ment in the creation of new theatres and arts centres.

## BURSARIES AND TRAINING SCHEMES

Gifted individuals in all branches of the arts can now look to the Council for the patronage which used to be supplied by the nobility or the wealthy who took such protégés under their wing. In drama, music, literature and art, bursaries and commissions are arranged on the strength of work and future plans submitted. Details are available from the appropriate departments.

## GENERAL SURVEYS

From time to time, the Panels of the various departments of the Council undertake fact-finding work and the resulting reports are of great value as a general conspectus of the world of the arts. In 1956 the Chancellor of the Exchequer invited the Arts Council to study the building needs for the arts in Great Britain. As a result of this survey, the two impressive volumes, *Housing the Arts in Great Britain*, Part I, "London, Scotland and Wales," in 1959 and Part II, "The English

Provinces," in 1961, were published. Topics such as the needs of the subsidized theatre in the provinces and in London, the future of Opera and Ballet, and theatre for young people have all received attention. A full inquiry into the condition of the theatre as a whole is currently in progress under the chairmanship of Sir William Emrys Williams, C.B.E., D.Litt., and promises to probe more deeply into all aspects of this topic than has ever been done before.

The Council is composed of members distinguished in many fields of the arts, with the terms of membership defined in the Charter. Each department is helped in its work by a panel of specialists, serving voluntarily and attending meetings with the officers of the special departments. Reports, recommendations, etc., go forward to the Council from the Panel about matters of policy and detail. Finance and its allocation are the concern of the officials of the departments, assisted in some of their proceedings by special sub-committees made up of members of the appropriate Panels and co-opted members where it is thought useful. The present scope of the Arts Council's work as a whole is indeed a great oak-tree from the acorn planted in 1939.

## 12

# ORGANIZATIONS CONNECTED
# WITH THEATRE

*The British Council,*
65 Davies Street, London, W.1.

The British Council was established in 1934 to promote cultural relations between Great Britain and countries overseas, for which purpose it receives subsidy from the Government. For the theatre, it promotes visits abroad by British companies, such as the Royal Shakespeare Company, the National Theatre and some of the major repertory companies. Countries visited include the USSR as a result of the setting-up of the Soviet Relations Committee in 1955. Its representatives all over the world help with the organization on the spot.

On the reception side in this country, overseas visitors are welcomed and directed to the places and people best able to further their particular interests. A training course for theatre people from abroad is held in London, conducted by experts from the British theatre world. There are centres and representatives of the Council in many of the major cities in the United Kingdom, notably University cities, to give help and advice to visitors and students from abroad and to provide a meeting place for them.

*The International Theatre Institute,*
The Archway, 10a Aquinas Street, London, S.E.1.

This body was set up by UNESCO to promote the international exchange of information about the theatre. It has centres in most countries abroad to receive foreign visitors and help them to plan tours of the theatres they wish to study, the

British Centre in London acting in the same way for visitors from abroad. The Institute is a valuable source of information about what is happening in contemporary theatre all over the world, supported by a copious interchange of periodicals, bulletins and the periodical, *World Theatre*, referred to on page 75. On its committee the British Centre has representatives of the Arts Council, the British Council, notable theatres and theatre organizations.

MANAGEMENT ORGANIZATIONS

*The Theatrical Management Association (TMA),*
Gloucester House, 19 Charing Cross Road, London, W.C.2.

This organization was founded in 1894 with Sir Henry Irving as its first president. It represents the interests of managements other than the London Theatres, for whom the Society of West End Managers was formed in 1908. Both bodies share offices and secretariat so that they are closely in touch as befits two bodies with much in common.

The membership is open to "Proprietors, Lessees, Licensees and Managers of theatres and places presenting live entertainment," so defined in the booklet *T.M.A. 1894–1963,* compiled by Mr. Geoffrey Robinson. The Association conveys the latest information to its members about Parliamentary measures affecting the theatre, particularly relevant in 1968 in the move to abolish the authority of the Lord Chamberlain and to examine the question of Sunday entertainment. One of its major functions is negotiations with the Trades Unions of the theatre, such as NATKE and the Musicians' Union. It is joined with the Association of Touring and Producing Managers and the Council of Repertory Theatres as the management side of the Provincial Theatre Council of which it became a member in 1942, to adopt and approve Esher Standard Contracts which must be used for the engagement of artists in the provinces.

The specialized aspects of its work are carried out by separate Committees whose meetings may be attended by any member with particular interests. The subscriptions payable are scaled according to the grading of the theatre, based on its status and seating capacity. Membership is by election, with proposer and seconder from among existing members, and a full member is entitled to Permanent Registration as an Approved Manager, able to enjoy all the privileges and good work done on behalf of the theatre by the TMA, both as a negotiating body and a source of information. It is a very necessary and powerful force in many spheres.

*Association of Touring and Producing Managers,*
18 Charing Cross Road, London, W.C.2.

This body, with membership from all sides of the entertainment industry including Equity, represents their interests in many of the management organizations described here. Information and problems relevant to this aspect of theatre management are studied.

*Provincial Theatre Council,*
Gloucester House, 19 Charing Cross Road, London, W.C.2.
*See TMA.*

The consortium of managerial bodies which approves and adopts contractual obligations between managers and artists in the theatres of the provinces and the London suburban area, excluding the West End. The Esher Standard Contracts so approved are the result of thorough discussion and negotiation with all the parties concerned.

*Theatres' Advisory Council (TAC),*
9–10 Fitzroy Square, London, W.1.

This is a comparatively recent organization formed in 1963 to represent and co-ordinate all theatre interests. These are wide and diverse—liaison with local authorities; advice on preserving and restoring existing buildings and guidance in projects for new ones; the collection and dissemination of information on the current situation about the numbers of existing theatres and proposals for new ones; and the provision of speakers on these matters.

*Standing Advisory Committee on Local Authorities and Theatre,*
9–10 Fitzroy Square, London, W.1.

This body was founded as a result of the work of the TAC, in conjunction with the Association of Municipal Corporations. Local authorities are kept informed of plans and projects, and meetings are arranged, sometimes on a regional basis, for the exchange of ideas and information.

*Theatres' National Committee,*
Gloucester House, 19 Charing Cross Road, London, W.C.2.

A consortium of the chief management organizations, representative of the society of West End Theatre Managers, the TMA, the Association of Touring and Producing Managers, the Association of Circus Proprietors of Great Britain and the Council of Repertory Theatres.

*Council of Repertory Theatres (CORT),*
9–10 Fitzroy Square, London, W.1.

The membership of this organization is open to non-profit-distributing managements of theatres in the provinces. This implies professional repertory theatres as distinct from the touring theatres owned commercially either by individuals or part of a circuit, such as Howard and Wyndham or Moss Empires. It exists primarily to examine and safeguard the interests of these companies, though "commercial" repertory companies may become Associate members by unanimous vote. Conferences are organized at 4-monthly intervals, which enable members from all over the country to meet for a timely and useful exchange of ideas and information, and to hear speakers on selected topics of special interest to promote discussion. It is therefore a most useful clearing house of ideas and plans, and works in association with the chief organizations described above. It is a constituent member of the Theatres' National Committee.

The CORT pamphlet, *The Repertory Movement in Great Britain* (1968) is an admirable source of information about the member theatres and the aims and work of the organization, with first-rate articles on repertory past and present.

## LOCAL AUTHORITIES AND THE THEATRE

With an increasing number of theatres coming under civic control there are at least two organizations for these particular interests—

*Institute of Municipal Entertainment,*
White Rock Pavilion, Hastings, Sussex

This body collects and disseminates relevant information for municipal entertainment in all its aspects. It devotes attention to the training of personnel for Entertainment Managers, whose duties include theatre, music and much else besides, particularly in holiday resorts and spas.

*Civic Entertainment Officers' Association,*
London Borough of Southwark, Entertainments Dept., 28 Peckham Road, London, S.E.5.

This, as its name makes clear, is an organization for those working in civic entertainment, and holds regular meetings in London to further this purpose.

## TRADES UNIONS AND OTHER ORGANIZATIONS (EQUITY)

*British Actors' Equity Association,*
8 Harley Street, London, W.1.

This organization for the acting profession was founded in 1929 and in 1967 the Variety Artistes' Federation was incorporated with it to form a single union for theatre performers. It was registered as a Trade Union in 1930 and negotiates with the appropriate bodies the terms of the contracts under which its members may be engaged. Members of Equity have the right to refuse to work with non-members. One member of a performing company is usually nominated as the Equity deputy to represent the company's views to the management should there appear to be cause for complaint or dispute. Equity has also representatives who visit theatres in various regions to meet the companies there and to see that all is in order *vis-à-vis* Equity's rules. The contracts cover all kinds of theatres and also the special conditions for British actors going on tours abroad. Equity has a strong voice also about the employment of foreign artists in the British theatre when work permits are required. Only when there is a very strong case for preferring a foreign to a British performer will Equity agree to this.

*National Association of Theatrical and Kine Employees (NATKE),*
20 Bedford Street, Strand, London, W.C.2.

Established in 1889, this body negotiates the terms of employment for the technical, craft and general staff in theatres and cinemas throughout Great Britain, and craft, administrative and general staff also in the studios of film and television. Standard contracts are agreed between NATKE and the appropriate management associations.

*Musicians' Union,*
29 Catherine Place, London, S.W.1.

This union is for musicians what Equity and NATKE are to their members, the trade union which negotiates agreements and conditions of employment with all bodies using musicians. It is affiliated to the Trade Union Congress and Labour Party as well as to many other organizations.

*West End Stage Management Association,*
81 St. Mary's Grove, London, W.1.

This is not a Trade Union but a strong association of stage managers working in the West End. It was formed in 1954 because the need was felt for a body to represent these interests. It also provides up-to-date information about availability to managements looking for staff. Out-of-town stage managements may become Associate members.

*Association of British Theatre Technicians (ABTT),*
9 Fitzroy Square, London, W.1.

This association was founded in 1961 for "all who assist the actor in a technical capacity." Its prime preoccupation therefore is with the developments in lighting technique, stage design, testing of new materials for the stage, the collection and collation of information about these and related topics. Its scope extends to the design and equipping of new theatres and all who are engaged in such projects are now recommended by the Arts Council, the TAC, and other bodies to seek advice from its committees of distinguished experts. Its bias is not wholly technical, however, and its Newsletter, issued several times a year, indicates its wide range of interests relating to most of what goes on in a theatre building excluding the actor, certainly everything connected with the staging of the production and the amenities and administration of the front of house. It has issued some useful reference books, *Theatre Planning 1 and 2*, in association with *The Architect's Journal*, in which the material was first published weekly as information sheets. Monthly meetings for members are held with guest speakers (occasionally from theatres in other countries), films and demonstrations.

*British Drama League (BDL),*
9 Fitzroy Square, London, W.1.

The BDL's aim is "to assist the development of the Art of the theatre and to promote a tight relation between drama and the life of the community."

More than 6,000 organizations benefit by affiliation with it and draw upon its many facilities. It is perhaps particularly helpful to amateur societies with its Bureau of Information and Advice and its vast library of plays and general works on everything connected with the theatre and drama. It provides adjudicators for amateur productions, and organizes Festivals of amateur drama which have a very high standard of production and presentation. Amateur directors can attend special training courses and study week-ends under the guidance of distinguished professional theatre people. The conferences organized under BDL auspices bring together amateurs, professionals, groups and individuals in valuable exchanges of experience and ideas. The League's illustrated journal *Drama*, which members receive free, keeps its readers up-to-date with articles, photographs, book reviews, and is a mine of general information and informed opinion about what is happening in the theatre.

Membership is open to groups and individuals, with an additional subscription for the Library (both separate volumes and reading sets are supplied).

*National Operatic and Dramatic Association (NODA),*
1 Crestfield Street, London, W.C.1.

This association is for amateur groups and individuals interested in amateur dramatic and operatic work. It gives advice and help to its members on the variety of matters involved in such productions and has a vast library of operatic and dramatic material. Its bulletin of information is published three times a year and its *Year Book* is a useful work of reference.

### ORGANIZATIONS REPRESENTING THE INTERESTS OF WRITERS AND COMPOSERS

*Performing Right Society,*
29–33 Berners Street, London, W.1.

Composers, authors and publishers are represented by this society, which collects on their behalf royalties and performance fees. It deals only with copyright musical works which are publicly performed or broadcast, excluding opera, musical plays or other dramatico-musical works given live on stage.

*Phonographic Performance Ltd.,*
Evelyn House, 62 Oxford Street, London, W.1.

Recorded music used for public performances is controlled by this body, whose members are virtually all the leading recording companies. All theatres which use such recordings, whether for overture or interval music, effects or part of a production, or item in a live show, must hold its licence. Licence fees are payable according to a tariff and returns must be made in detail of all records used.

*Society of Authors,* and
*League of Dramatists;*
both at 84 Drayton Gardens, London, S.W.10.

The Society was founded in 1884 for the protection of

authors' interests and to help them with legal and general advice.

The League was founded in 1931 by the Society for the special interests of the work of dramatists, particularly their contracts with theatre managements, negotiation of royalties, etc.

*Writers' Guild of Great Britain,*
430 Edgware Road, London, W.2.

The Guild concentrates on work for writers for film, television, radio and advertising. It is a member also of the International Workers' Guild.

*Note.* There are, of course, many other organizations representing special sections of the complex theatre community, to say nothing of the charitable concerns and benevolent funds. A good and exhaustive summary is included in *The Stage Year Book*, and detailed up-to-date information about the activities of all such organizations should be sought from their secretaries.

# 13

# THEATRE PUBLICATIONS

IT is a little hazardous to set out at any time a list of current periodicals without saying that this is subject to change, decay and mergers. At the date of writing the following periodicals appear to be flourishing. The categories are not rigid demarcations since a lot of material is common to many.

### CURRENT THEATRE

*The Stage and Television Today.* A weekly newspaper with reviews, news of regional theatre, proposed productions and an important advertising section. 19–21 Tavistock Street, London, W.C.2.

*Plays and Players.* A monthly magazine incorporating *Theatre World* and *Encore*, *Play Pictorial*, and *Shows Illustrated*. Photographs of current productions, reviews and articles. Scripts of new plays. Published by Hansom Books Ltd., 16 Buckingham Palace Road, London, S.W.1.

*Opera.* A monthly magazine devoted to international opera. Articles, reviews of books and records, with photographs. Published by Rolls House Publishing Co. Ltd., Rolls House, Breams Buildings, London, E.C.4.

*Amateur Stage.* A monthly magazine dealing with every aspect of the amateur theatre. Informative and instructive articles, news, views and reviews. Published by Stacey Publications, 1 Hawthorndene Road, Hayes, Bromley, Kent.

### CRITICAL WORK

*Tulane Drama Review.* An American publication with scholarly critical and historical articles, comment on current American theatre and book reviews. An issue is often devoted to a special subject, e.g. Brecht, Film and Theatre, or to the drama of one country. Published quarterly by Tulane University under the auspices of its Department of Theatre and Speech. Address, Tulane University, New Orleans, Louisiana 70118.

*Educational Theatre Journal.* Published quarterly for members of the American Educational Theatre Association Inc. Scholarly articles of general interest on European and American theatre. Published at the John F. Kennedy Centre, 1701 Pennsylvania Avenue, N.W., Washington, D.C.

*World Theatre.* A bi-monthly review published by the International Theatre Institute with the assistance of UNESCO. Parallel text in French and English. Reports on theatre all over the world, sometimes concentrated on a special subject, such as Theatre in France, Total Theatre, etc., with reports of current productions in many countries and of international conferences. Well illustrated with photographs. Published by Editeurs Michel Birent, 64 Rue de Saintonge, Paris 3.

*Italian Theatre Review.* The bulletin of the Italian National Theatre Guild, Via del Titone 132, Rome. Contains the text of recent Italian plays, in Italian, French and English, also news of Italian theatre and comment on productions and theatre in many countries.

*Gambit.* Published quarterly in association with Calder and Boyars Ltd., 18 Brewer Street, London, W.1. Gives the texts of interesting and little-known plays. English or in translation. Plans for expansion are being made with the publishing firm of Calder & Boyars Ltd., to continue to draw attention to unusual new work, and also to include features on new productions on the Continent.

## HOUSE MAGAZINES

*About the House.* The magazine of the Friends of the Royal Opera House, Covent Garden. Beautifully produced glossy magazine with articles on current operas, composers, etc., lavishly illustrated.

*Flourish.* The newspaper-format paper issued to members of the Royal Shakespeare Theatre Club. Articles on matters of current theatre interest, related but not confined to the productions by the Royal Shakespeare Theatre at Stratford and the Aldwych Theatre.

The programmes of the Royal Shakespeare Company productions deserve a mention. They are lavishly produced, with articles on the play, its history and background, etc., together with rehearsal and production photographs. They have an interest and usefulness beyond the occasion of a visit to the play. All this applies also to the programmes of the National Theatre. In both cases, cast lists are given free. The full programme is a separate publication for those who want an informative brochure.

*New Theatre Magazine.* Issued by the Department of Drama of the University of Bristol. Articles on general theatrical topics and matters related to the Drama Department productions.

*Prompt.* Published three times a year by University College London Drama Society, University College, Gower Street, London, W.C.1.

### PERIODICALS ISSUED BY SOCIETIES AND OTHER SPECIALIST BODIES

*Theatre Notebook.* Includes the Bulletin of the Society for Theatre Research. Articles on aspects of the theatre and drama revealed by recent research or work in progress. The address of the Society for Theatre Research is: 103 Ralph Court, Queensway, London, W.2.

*Costume.* The journal of the Costume Society (founded in 1965), care of Department of Textiles, Victoria and Albert Museum, London, S.W.7. It is issued from time to time with articles on design and costume generally, accompanied by pattern sketches with instructions for cutting and making historical costume.

*ABTT Newsletter.* The bulletin of the Association of British Theatre Technicians. Contains articles on technical matters of current interest—new buildings, the use of new materials in the theatre, controversy about all these topics, etc. Issued from the ABTT, 9 Fitzroy Square, London, W.1.

*Tabs.* Issued by the Strand Electric and Engineering Co. Ltd., 29 King Street, Covent Garden, London, W.C.2. Contains articles and reports on the technical aspects, not restricted to lighting, of new buildings, details of new equipment, special devices used in current productions for lighting, scenery, etc. Also carries information about special lectures on lighting and related topics held on the premises of the firm in their demonstration theatre.

*Drama.* The quarterly magazine of the British Drama League, issued monthly. Contains a regular feature about current productions in London and notable events in the provinces, a great deal of space devoted to book reviews, useful information about suppliers of lighting, costumes, scenery, etc., for amateur productions. Issued from The British Drama League, 9 Fitzroy Square, London, W.1.

### GENERAL INFORMATION

*The Arts Council Reports* issued annually are an indispensable source of information about the bird's-eye-view of the progress of theatre in Britain. They contain also details of the subsidies given to the arts through the channel of the Council and are often illustrated by the work of well-known artists.

Their exhibition catalogues for past and current exhibitions are available, together with special reports such as that on Housing the Arts.

*The Architectural Review.* This monthly periodical often contains articles on new theatre buildings, with good photographs and details of the plans of the stage. For theatre people who have an insatiable curiosity about other people's "houses," these articles are of great interest. Published by the Architectural Press Ltd., 9–13 Queen Anne's Gate, London, S.W.1.

*Architects' Journal.* Gives a weekly survey of architectural matters and features new buildings of all types, including theatres. Collaborated with ABTT in the issue of *Theatre Planning*, a detailed examination of the problems involved. Also published by the Architectural Press Ltd.

### REFERENCE BOOKS

*Who's Who in the Theatre.* Gives information about people, theatres and plays, dates of productions, etc. An inexhaustible source of detail and dates, admirably set out and indexed for easy reference. Published by Sir Isaac Pitman & Sons Ltd. (Not at present in stock but can be consulted in various libraries.)

*The Stage Year Book*, published annually by Carson & Comerford Ltd., proprietors of *The Stage*, 19–21 Tavistock Street, London, W.C.2. Contains articles on current theatre topics, photographs of each year's productions, alphabetical list of plays presented each year, with cast lists, and all the professional lists, contract details, etc., one could wish for.

*Spotlight Casting Directory.* Two editions a year of this *vade mecum* to the world of actors and actresses. Indispensable for casting purposes. Available from Spotlight Ltd., 43 Cranbourn Street, London, W.C.2.

*Contacts.* Produced quarterly by the publishers of Spotlight Casting Directory. A handy reference book for addresses and telephone numbers of theatres, London and provincial, agents, managers, suppliers, and related interests.

*Oxford Companion to the Theatre.* Published by the Oxford University Press, this covers an incredibly wide range of theatre information. Most useful for historical and literary background.

This list makes no claim to be exhaustive or anywhere near complete but merely indicates those sources which are useful in day-to-day reference for general theatre purposes.

*Part Two*
Administration

# 14

## COMPANY FORMATION

All theatre companies eligible to receive subsidy from the Arts Council are registered under the Companies Acts 1948 to 1967 as limited by guarantee and not having a share capital. The Memorandum and Articles of Association should be drawn up by a solicitor and must be carefully framed. For those who wish to set up a bona-fide company operating in this way the Arts Council provides a useful model on request, which may be varied in some details for special requirements but which covers the salient points. The most important of these are as follows—

1. *The Main Object*, which is defined in a phrase such as "to present, promote, organize, maintain, improve and advance education particularly by the production of plays and the arts including drama, puppet shows, broadcasts, ballet, music, singing, entertainments, literature, sculpture, painting." Companies pursuing such objects by these means may be registered as Charities, with the benefits accruing from such registration.

2. *Operation.* The furthering of the main objects is elaborately defined to include the acquisition of copyright, the purchasing or acquisition of premises, the acceptance of gifts, the borrowing and raising of money investment under the jurisdiction of the Charity Commissioners, donations to other charities, etc.

3. *Disbursements.* It is important that some categories of expenditure should be specified, particularly agreements with artists and performers in every field of the company's activity, advisers to be reimbursed, pension schemes, the costs of forming and registering the company, "reasonable and proper remuneration" to the directors or "other officers or servants of the Company," not only for services actually rendered. Such expenditure and payments to individuals

are allowed provided that the income and property of the company are applied solely to promoting the objects of the company, with no distribution of profit to the members.

4. *Members and Directors.* The number of the members and directors of the company is specified, together with the conduct of meetings, keeping of minutes, General Meeting, preparation of the balance sheet, etc. The manner of appointing chairman and secretary and the rotation of the directors in tenure of office are also laid down.

An important administrative detail is the procedure for signing cheques and the number of directors' signatures required. This must be carefully planned so that the management is never left stranded without an available director.

It is important for companies receiving subsidy from the Arts Council to note that in addition to the stipulations of the Company's Memorandum and Articles of Association they must observe certain other conditions laid down by the Council. These follow on the acceptance by the Council of the management as properly constituted as a non-profit-distributing Company or a charitable trust. An Arts Council assessor is entitled to attend Board meetings, and to insist on such meetings being regularly held at stated intervals. A copy of the minutes must be sent to the Council, together with such estimates of income and expenditure, statements of actual figures and any other information about the company's operation as they may require and whenever they request them. It requires consultation with the Council before special projects, such as tours abroad, participation by an employee in the rights of a production, are undertaken. The Council requires a copy of the audited annual Balance Sheet issued by the company.

## REGISTRATION OF A THEATRICAL EMPLOYER

A new company setting itself up for the purposes outlined above must also be registered with the Local Authority. The requirements vary in different areas, but the application form will give the necessary details. The responsible administrator should then seek membership of the Theatrical Management Association.

# 15

## BOARDS OF MANAGEMENT

IT is usual for the administration of a theatre to be responsible to a Board of Management. The pattern on which these
boards are formed varies greatly according to the status and
the situation of the theatre and of course its ownership.
The central facts common to them all is that the members
receive no remuneration and that they are usually elected or
appointed to represent particular facets of local interests as
well as for their individual contributions. The relation between the board and their key employees, the Artistic Director
and Administrator, is therefore a rather delicate one, and one
which has to be worked out in terms of personalities.

There is no hard and fast pattern to be recommended
overall, but from common experience one or two conclusions
may be drawn.

The first is the determining of the precise relationship of the
Board members to the professionals who formulate the artistic
policy of the theatre and who do the day-to-day work. They
may regard themselves as advisory only, in which case, if they
have confidence in the staff appointed on their authority, they
may be happy to demonstrate this confidence by allowing them
a comparatively free hand.

This confidence should create in the Artistic Director and the
Administrator the responsibility to keep the Board fully informed on all matters of policy and finance. The mainspring
of efficient and pleasant working can well hinge on this mutual
trust, and, if the Board is too large and its members too occu-
pied with other things to wish to hear everything in detail,
a small management committee to meet with the Artistic
Director and Administrator at frequent and regular intervals
can well act as a bridge.

The matter of information brings us to the setting up and
conduct of the meetings, so that the discussions can be as fully
documented as possible. Points to be borne in mind—

## DATES OF MEETINGS

It is very difficult to bring together all the members of any body regularly at any one time convenient to them all. The best solution is to fix a regular pattern and to settle the dates as far ahead as possible. For theatre business, where reversal can take the place of estimated success virtually overnight, these regular meetings should also be as frequent as possible, either at the end of each production in a repertory season or, if the schedule is not so regular, say every month.

## MINUTES

The registered company (the producing management) may have a secretary who keeps the minutes and sets up meetings, but this may fall to the lot of the Administrator. It is in any case a company rule that such minutes must be fully and correctly kept. If the company has a subsidy from the Arts Council copies of the minutes must be sent to the Council as well as to all members of the Board. The minute book kept for the company must have all the minutes stuck in and signed by the chairman of the meeting at which they are read and adopted.

For purposes of easy reference it is a good idea to head each minute with the subject matter and to number them consecutively regardless of the divisions into separate meetings. The meetings should also be numbered, so that it is easy to find a particular reference, e.g. "Minute No. 301 in the Minutes of the 20th Meeting" is easier to track in a wad of papers than "Minute No. 3 of the meeting held on January 3, 1967."

## OTHER MATERIAL

Since it is often ignorance or the feeling of not having been informed which creates suspicion and ill-feeling, as much material as possible should be circulated before the meeting to all the members of the board for consideration under the appropriate heading of the agenda. Time is an important factor. Material of great importance, such as estimates of income and expenditure, must reach the Board as long as possible before the meeting at which they are to be considered. Box-office results, profit and loss estimates on production accounts, even if not finally accurate to the last penny, should be sent round as soon as possible. Minutes of the smaller working committee, if such exists, should be as full as possible, to save further elaboration verbally at the meeting.

It is a time-saving matter too to set out the pros and cons of a controversial matter, e.g. proposed increases in staff salaries, in a preliminary paper. A verbal report may be too discursive to be taken in at the first hearing and arguments may lose their impact through interjections or questions while the facts are being given. Such papers and indeed all documents should be given a title for easy reference, e.g. Paper A (Box-office results) Paper B (Estimates 1968/9) and so on. All that makes for quick reference enables the meetings to be used to the best advantage.

### PRELIMINARY CONSULTATION

Time is never wasted in a preliminary meeting between the Chairman of the board and the key staff who attend the board meetings. This is not the "lobbying" it is sometimes suspected of being, but reasonable guidance for the Chairman. He has somehow to guide a number of persons who are not all necessarily well-informed about the theatre to make the conclusions which he and the professionals think are right. He may himself actually know little compared with a professional but must interest himself sufficiently to understand what the professionals are after and to assure himself of the rightness of their aims and methods. His colleagues probably have known prejudices and the pre-marshalling of arguments by consultation before a meeting is very helpful. In every meeting the importance of keeping an eye on the clock so that no crucial business is omitted for lack of time is vital to the progress of affairs. This is not to say that the Chairman should ride roughshod over his colleagues. What he must do is to sense the happy medium between prolonged rambling off the subject and the useful exchange of views which makes everyone happy that his voice has been heard, even if it has not been applauded. In short, the Chairman must be a man of diplomacy, clarity of mind, tact and patience.

He is the figurehead and the spokesman for the company and often has to speak for the theatre in negotiations with public bodies—the Arts Council, local authorities, etc. If it can attract and keep as its Chairman a knowledgeable man who is respected and well-known in the community, and who trusts and is trusted by the professional theatre staff, it has a very enviable asset, and is likely to be a successful enterprise with a harmonious and creative atmosphere. The amalgam of interests represented in a theatre Board is by no means easy to achieve. Each "side," the professional theatre people and the business men and local dignitaries, have to learn to respect each other's qualities and to resist the pressure of vested interests. Difficulties can arise when the Board is self-perpetuating or when its members do not retire in a rotation geared to take in new blood. These problems have been brought to the notice of the Arts Council which is in process of examining their implications. Any body proposing to operate in a theatre should be very careful in the initial stages of setting up a company, and on this crucial point the Arts Council's advice is invaluable.

# 16

## THE STAFF STRUCTURE
## OF A THEATRE WITH
## RESIDENT COMPANY

STEMMING from the two king-pins of the theatre—the Artistic Director and the General Manager or Administrator, the currently fashionable term—there are two interlocking areas of responsibility.

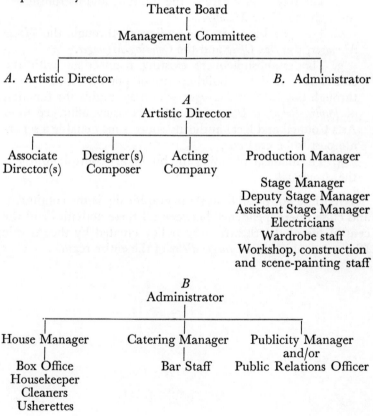

Theatre Board
|
Management Committee
|

*A.* Artistic Director                    *B.* Administrator

*A*
Artistic Director
|

Associate        Designer(s)        Acting          Production Manager
Director(s)      Composer           Company         |
                                                    Stage Manager
                                                    Deputy Stage Manager
                                                    Assistant Stage Manager
                                                    Electricians
                                                    Wardrobe staff
                                                    Workshop, construction
                                                    and scene-painting staff

*B*
Administrator
|

House Manager          Catering Manager        Publicity Manager
|                      |                        and/or
Box Office             Bar Staff               Public Relations Officer
Housekeeper
Cleaners
Usherettes

It must be emphasized, however, that there are few hard-and-fast limitations of the duties of most of the people concerned.

It is no accident that the Artistic Director's responsibility leads on directly to the production activity. The production team is a large one, covering rehearsing, scenery, lighting, costumes, props—everything appertaining to the physical production on the stage. It is mainly concentrated within the theatre and is supervised by the heads of each department, each with his assistants, correlated overall by the Production Manager.

The Administrator's responsiblity is spread out widely into the departments of the theatre which can be divided into four main categories—

1. The day-to-day care of the building and its routines—through the *House Manager*.

2. The provision for the audience—through the *House Manager*, the *Box Office* and the *Catering Manager*.

3. The establishment of existing connections with the community and the building up of potential audiences—through the *Publicity Manager*, who may double the function of *Public Relations Officer* (though increasing affluence from Arts Council and local authority sources may enable a separate post to be created).

4. The financial planning and budgetary control—through the *Accountant*.

What it is not possible to show graphically is the continuous and close interdependence between all these activities and the central life of the theatre—the policy created by the Artistic Director—which is the *raison d'être* of the entire régime.

# 17

# THE ARTISTIC DIRECTOR
# AND HIS STAFF

THE Artistic Director is finally and often personally responsible for the policy of the theatre. His choice of plays embodies
the particular character of the theatre, based on a combination
of personal predilection and a sense of what is acceptable to
his audience. This is a difficult assignment, since giving the
public what it wants may lead to a depressingly low standard
in choice of plays, and feeding it with a diet of new or difficult
plays may alienate this public and reduce the box office. It
needs great artistic integrity and a strong sense of dedication
to the gradual and often discouragingly slow task of widening
horizons and consolidating achievement.

Emphatically, the Artistic Director must not be divorced at
any point from the administration. Equally with the Administrator he should be able to assess the evidence of the box-office
returns night by night and over a whole season; to budget
the costs of his productions as accurately as possible, aside from
the hazards of inexplicable public caprice; to think and plan
ahead for the season after next to carry the achievement of
the theatre well into the future. How exacting this is can be
realized when day by day he must take rehearsals, cast his
plays, consult with his designers and technical staff, and meet
the demands for speaking at local functions, fulfilling his social-
professional duties. Above all he must be constantly reading
plays, both those he may wish to produce and the shoals which
are sent by would-be new dramatists. Theatres in the provinces cannot, alas, afford the continental practice of having a
full-time dramaturge or literary adviser. There is the constant
nightmare of missing an important new play through sheer
lack of time for reading. In these conditions, even periods
when the theatre is closed may become a busman's holiday—
the only chance of seeing productions in other theatres, either

at home or abroad, or of catching up with a backlog of plays to be read.

The post of Artistic Director of a company or theatre is much coveted in spite of its tough demands. The few who achieve it have usually served an apprenticeship of years of directing plays at many other theatres of various kinds and in all conditions. Direction may be preceded by an earlier period of work in stage management or other technical departments. The more general knowledge of the theatre and of its technical branches he has been able to amass, the better. If along the way the Director has also been able to act as company manager, to work with a company on tour or in any way to acquire some knowledge of finance and administration, the stronger he will be. Above all he must have perception, the imagination to make his theatre a distinctive entity and the practical ability to use these gifts to the full.

### THE DESIGNER

The designer works with the director to interpret his ideas for the visual side of the production and to give him the kind of acting area which will best serve his image of the play. When the set has been planned, consultation then ensues with the administrator and the production manager to check the costing. It is usual to indicate to a designer the sum of money he is allowed. It is important to indicate to him at this preliminary stage of the proceedings whether it has to include dressings and furniture, as well as the flats, rostra, etc., so that misunderstanding should not arise when it is too late. A check on the costing when the set plans are submitted is essential, while there is still time to make alterations or retrenchments. The Stage Manager should be included in a conference to comment on the method of running the production.

A scale model of the set should then be made for most careful checking by the director and the production manager. Working drawings then follow for use by the construction staff. The painting may be done by the designer himself, as some prefer to do, or deputed to chosen and trained assistants.

Constant supervision during the construction and painting

is usually undertaken by the designer, and the whole set remains his responsibility until the production has opened. If he is also required to make further changes after the opening, this possibility must be mentioned in the agreement made with him by the management. It is customary to pay a proportion of a designer's fee when he submits the designs and model, and the remainder after the first night. The agreement must be made before work begins and should be very specific about the details of time and requirements and exactly what is included in the money involved, e.g. distinguish between fee and expenses, if these are not included in the fee; state the ceiling of expenses for essential travel and accommodation if a limit has to be set; state whether all or any of the materials needed in realizing the design drawings and model are to be paid for by the management, and if so, to what extent.

### THE LIGHTING DESIGNER

He is responsible for the artistic co-ordination of lighting effects with scenery and costumes, working closely with the director to interpret his wishes in practical terms. When the lighting plot is made to the liking of the director and himself, it is handed over for operation during performances by the theatre electricians.

If the company tours, the lighting designer works with the Production Manager to ascertain how closely the original intention can be carried out with differing conditions and equipment.

### THE COMPOSER

The composer of any incidental music required must be treated rather like the designer. He will be required to interpret the director's wishes in musical idiom as required. They will together decide on the points in the action where music is required and how long these passages of music should last.

It is essential in the agreement made between the composer and the management to crystallize these requirements, to estimate the cost of copying the music, paying the musicians for recording sessions and hiring the premises in which the recordings may best be made. The areas of fee and expenses must be defined as for the director, and the question of ownership and copyright must be decided.

### THE PRODUCTION TEAM

There should be no gulf fixed between one side of the curtain and the other, and while the Administrator delegates much of his authority to the technical experts, these are not a race apart. The two sides are complementary, the two parts of the operation to bring the spectacle to the public, and both should know and understand each other's work and functions.

### THE PRODUCTION MANAGER

He is the closest to the administration and a participant in the overall planning of the work. As the leader of the stage team he carries out in detail the policy agreed by the management. He is responsible for deploying the technicians directly under his control and checks the budget expenditure allocated to the stage departments for each production. Information about these matters should be fully discussed with him by the Artistic Director and the Administrator. When all are satisfied that reasonable finance, rehearsal arrangements and production plans have been made, it is the Production Manager's task to exercise leadership and control backstage, similar to that of the Administrator front of the house. He is in fact the coordinator. The actual running of the show is deputed to his staff, while he begins the forward planning for the next production.

If the programme involves touring, he will obtain stage plans and specifications of equipment from the touring theatres, arrange for the transport of the production and possibly organize the get-in and fit-up there, organize special effects, etc., working as far ahead as possible. It is helpful if he can visit the touring theatres in advance, at least before the company's first visit, so as to get to know the staff and general organization in each place. At all times and in all the arrangements he is responsible for checking the expenditure on productions and presenting the accounts, based on certified sub-accounts from wardrobe, electrics, stage-management, etc., to the administrator.

## THE STAGE MANAGER

He is in charge of the stage and company throughout the running of the show. The various tasks of stage-management—giving out of personal properties, setting of properties on the stage-scene, prompting, and cueing the electrics and the flies from the prompt corner—are allocated by him to the other members of the stage-management. He is responsible for the conduct of rehearsals, which involve the following procedures, also carried out by the stage-management team as allocated—

1. *Making the prompt-copy*, a copy of the play dismembered so that it can be interleaved with blank pages. On these are written notes of the actors' moves, cues for their entrances, cues for sound and lighting effects and for the flymen. This document, efficiently annotated, is the key to the smooth running of the production from the prompt-corner, which has usually communication by inter-comm. to the dressing-rooms for calling the actors and to the flies, sound and electric boxes. There are usually warning bells also for the front of the house, so that bar staff and usherettes are ready at their various posts before the interval. The prompt copy should be in use from the beginning of rehearsals.

2. *Setting up the rehearsal room.* A member of the stage-management team should be responsible for marking out on the floor of the rehearsal room the acting area, indications of doors, rostra, etc., before the set is in use. This is done by putting down coloured tape with drawing pins or adhesive tape, according to the floor surface. Properties needing to be used in the course of the action must be provided as early as possible in the rehearsal period, with the necessary furniture. These may or may not be the ones to be used in the production, but should be as nearly equivalent as can be provided.

3. *Installing the production in the theatre.* The Stage Manager supervises the get-in and fit-up with his own team and that of the resident theatre, if the company is on tour, working under his direction. He allocates the dressing-rooms, which should be indicated by a neatly-written or typed card, with a list in the Green Room for reference.

4. *Checking the running of the show.* When the first night is over the production should settle down to run nightly to the same timing. The running time of each act must be entered in a special book kept in the prompt-corner and signed by the Stage Manager nightly, together with any comments on untoward happenings, number of curtain calls, and reasons for any delay or incident causing variation in the timing. While not himself doing any specific job in the running of the show, he will supervise all scene-changes, check the stage and keep in touch with the front of house for the signal to raise the curtain.

The other members of the stage-management team are the Deputy Stage Manager, Assistant Stage Managers, and students if any. Their work is allocated by the Stage Manager according to their experience and aptitudes co-ordinated with the demands of the production. Shows which are particularly elaborate may need casual staff for performances only, if there are more properties and more elaborate scene-changes than can be handled by the regular staff. Their number and functions are decided by the Stage Manager, and he is responsible for collecting their time-sheets for payment.

## THE WARDROBE MISTRESS

She works closely with the designer whether or not she is responsible for the actual making of the costumes. It is her responsibility to organize costume-fittings for each member of the cast before the first dress-rehearsal. She is responsible for all accessories, wigs and shoes, etc. With the designer and production manager she decides what, if anything, must be hired and is then responsible for the hiring and the final return of costumes.

During the running of the show, she must be present to see that all the costumes are always clean, correct and complete. Washing and ironing and dressing of wigs must be organized so that no actor goes on in damp clothes or with an unkempt coiffure. Running repairs are constantly needed for minor damage caused by the fumbling of nervous and impatient fingers or violent action on stage.

On tour she is particularly needed to see that costumes are neatly packed, that nothing is left out and that the costumes are all pressed and fresh before the first night. She may need to organize and instruct dressers both at home and away, especially if quick changes are needed.

### THE COMPANY AND STAGE MANAGER ON TOUR

While the Administrator is responsible for the initial contracts for a tour, the conduct of affairs and the day-to-day routine while the company is touring are in the hands of the Company and Stage Manager. He has this elaborate title because he is required to combine administrative and stage management qualifications. Some of his duties in these categories are as follows—

1. *As Company Manager* he is, as the title implies, in charge of the Company. He is responsible for imparting to them all the travel arrangements, paying their salaries, calling them to rehearsals and generally supervising their welfare and sorting out their problems. He is also the representative of the management in dealings with the resident managements of the theatres visited. Strictly speaking, and reverting to the practice generally accepted when there was a Stage Director as well as a Company Manager, he should be front of house during the half hour while the public enters. The box-office returns should be checked nightly. He should pass on to the box office all requests for tickets from his company. He should also help entertain visitors who are particularly the concern of his own management, e.g. West End managers assessing the potential of the show, agents, and anyone else who has a special interest in the production. He should also agree the final settlement, contra account, etc., at the end of the engagement.

2. *As Stage Manager* he is responsible for planning and supervising the arrangements for getting the production in, consulting and working with the resident staff. He may also have to light the show. If the management is fortunate enough to employ a permanent Production Manager, lighting plots, ground plans, etc., will have been prepared and sent ahead as part of the Production Manager's job. In most cases, however, this forward planning will also have fallen to the lot of the Company and Stage Manager. If he is a good one, and has learnt from experience, he will know that the more information can be supplied in advance, particularly of special effects and requirements, the smoother the get-in will be, and, very important, the quicker! Time, especially on Sunday at double rates, is certainly money.

He will be backstage throughout the first performance, fitting this in with his front-of-house duties. Thereafter, if the show runs smoothly and has already been in production for some time, he will turn his attention during the day to the same routine for the next date; the planning, the checking of arrangements made earlier by his office at the home base, the sending off of advance publicity and photographs, keeping his management supplied with copies of the nightly returns, press notices, calling understudy rehearsals, etc. During the performances he will keep an eye on the show, have chats with actors whose morale may sink under the strain of touring, take rehearsals if need be to freshen the performance, and plan the work of his staff.

In fact, the job of the touring Company and Stage Manager is no sinecure. It calls for exceptional organizing ability, the habit of forethought, patience and the ability to keep happy both his company and the staff of the theatres he visits. These qualities are not easy to maintain in unceasing adjustment to different people and conditions. There are those to whom the nomadic life appeals, and if they also have the necessary qualities and the technical knowledge they are worth their weight in gold.

### General Note

For the well-being and success of any theatre it is essential that the production and backstage team must be a harmonious whole. They are dovetailed, artistically and financially, with the Artistic Director (who will often in a regularly operating company be the Director of the play or will select a guest director of his choice) and the Administrator. The Administrator's paramount duty is to see that the organization of a production is efficient overall, that proper preparations are being made by all the staff concerned and that the expenditure is going as planned. He must be assured before all concerned embark on it that everything has been thought of and that so far as is possible the foundations are correctly laid. It is here that experience or at least some knowledge of the work of all departments stands him in good stead. No one minds being questioned, but the query goes down better if it springs from reasonable doubt or curiosity rather than the panic of ignorance.

## 18

## THE ADMINISTRTAOR
## AND HIS STAFF

THE term "Administrator" is widely used in preference to
General Manager, partly perhaps because the term "Manager"
occurs in other contexts, e.g. House Manager, Publicity
Manager.

The Administrator should be the practical complement of
the Artistic Director and this conjunction of two people able to
work closely and amicably together is fundamental to the
creation of a lively theatre with a distinctive policy. Taking
for granted the tenet that the Administrator must be able to
translate ideas into practical terms, he must be competent in
the following skills—

### FINANCE

This is finally the life-blood of the theatre, and all planning
and running must be based on an efficient financial policy.
This includes the following points—

1. Budgets must be made for annual expenditure and income, covering all the needs of the theatre—overhead costs
and production expenditure.

2. For each play the budget for heads of departments
must be broken down and agreed in detail. A watch on
expenditure must then be constantly kept.

3. The financial terms of contracts with other companies
and bodies using the theatre must be settled by negotiation,
since there are few set formulae which cover every case
and contingency.

4. The rates of pay for various departments have to be
aligned and settled.

The Administrator can do all this with the co-operation of

the Accountant if there is one, but certainly in amateur companies and small professional companies he may have to deal with everything himself, from a contact with a West End manager to such matters as Selective Employment Tax and overtime.

(More guidance on this basic duty is given in the chapter on Theatre Finance, pages 158–86.)

### LEGAL RESPONSIBILITIES

These fall into categories—

1. To the *Local Authority* of the city in which the theatre is situated, as defined in the Theatre Licence for the building and conduct within it.

2. To the *Police*, who have the right to enforce the conditions of the licence. There are also regulations regarding the use of fire-arms, overnight working in the theatre and many others.

3. To the *Fire Authorities*, who, with the Police, have the right to check the building, the carrying out of fire-drill, etc.

4. To the *Local Authority* in matters such as the employment of children, building alterations, etc.

5. To *Customs and Excise*, for the licensed sale of beers, wines and spirits.

6. To *Professional Associations and Trades Unions* as applicable to all employees.

7. To *Agents* and holders of copyright for plays and for payments in this connection, and to actors' agents in the negotiation of salaries and contracts.

### PUBLIC RELATIONS

The inclusion of a publicity or Public Relations Office in the staff of a theatre does not by any means exclude the Administrator from final responsibility for the "image" (to use a convenient, if overworked term) of the theatre. This responsibility is of two kinds.

Firstly, in the local community the Administrator should be a well-known figure and should participate as actively as possible in its life. It may well seem that all twenty-four hours of the day are adequately disposed of in carrying out all the other duties and demands of the job. Even so, time must be found, and cheerfully, for talking to local groups, showing parties round the theatre, showing the flag at local functions and getting to know other workers in related fields—education, music, art, local government. He must be articulate about the policy of the theatre and able to answer detailed if often irrelevant questions about the plays. In fact, he must be available and accessible—perhaps qualities of temperament rather than tangible qualification, but they are of primary importance.

Secondly, within his own domain he must have the respect of his staff. He may be a beast since in some theatre staff of the old school "management" is regarded as a natural enemy, but he must also and always be a just beast. While it is too demanding to expect him to be a glorified personnel officer, he must be considerate of his staff as individuals and also keenly aware of the demands of their work. Then labour problems should not arise, or, if they do, can be coped with amicably before they reach exaggerated proportions.

The Administrator should never be a complete Pooh-Bah and must delegate definite areas of his work to his assistants. First among these is—

### THE HOUSE MANAGER (OFTEN ASSISTANT MANAGER)

He should be immediately recognizable by the audience, which is the reason why he usually wears a dinner-jacket for the performance. He should be in the foyer before performances to welcome the audience and to be a mine of information for all the questions theatre patrons tend to ask—about parking, eating after the show, the temperature of the theatre and so on *ad infinitum* (but never, for the House Manager, please, *ad nauseam*). He may even be asked to mind dogs or babies during the show. This pre-performance appearance is not, however, as some people naïvely think, the sum total of his job. His responsibilities are many.

1. THE ADMINISTRATOR'S UNDERSTUDY

A lively Administrator who is involved in the theatre generally, and in the life of other theatres, may find it necessary to be away quite often. In order that the current of affairs may not be broken, the House Manager should be ready to carry on. He should therefore be in the Administrator's confidence about all theatre business and able either intelligently to continue negotiations in progress or to take in the import of further inquiries to report to the Administrator.

2. PUBLIC RELATIONS

He can usefully share the tasks of talking to local groups, etc., and if there is no P.R.O. to organize party bookings should keep in touch with schools, etc., to develop the theatre's sphere of influence.

3. TRAINEESHIP

This post can well be regarded as the final step towards that of Administrator proper and in many theatres it is now a useful habit to regard it as a trainee post. The contacts which he gains through working closely with the Administrator are the best foundation for learning the know-how of management. There is no substitute in any theoretical training so effective as actually having to do the many jobs for which he will be called upon.

4. STAFF RELATIONS

The House Manager will usually have special responsibility to several other departments and categories of staff.

### (i) *Box Office*

In many theatres he is required to check the box-office receipts nightly against the ticket plans, check the floats and either help with the banking of the cash or indeed be responsible for it. This is particularly important in a theatre used by visiting companies, with whose Company Manager he should be in close co-operation.

### (ii) *Front-of-house Amenities*

Circulation in the intervals can be of valuable assistance to the Administrator. The House Manager should keep an eye on the service in the bars, and be ready to deflect staff from one place to another if queues develop for, say, ice-cream or coffee, which may make patrons irritated and fearful that they will not be served in time to enjoy at least a part of the interval before they return to their seats. It is not too mundane to say that he must even be ready to suggest to patrons that there are other lavatories (as one hopes) in the theatre, if long queues develop. This is particularly necessary in schools performances when children may be too timid or sheep-like to explore the other possibilities of the building for themselves. He is also responsible to the Administrator for seeing that the licence regulations about exits, lighting, etc., are fulfilled.

### (iii) *Cleaners*

Cleaners are valued members of any theatre's staff. They share in a unique position of trust, since naturally all parts of the theatre—offices, dressing rooms, food store-rooms, technical rooms with valuable equipment, etc., must be open to them, usually without supervision. Actors can be notably careless with their possessions, and not all the management's documents can always be under lock and key. Trusted cleaners must therefore be treasured and their interests watched. On behalf of the Administrator, it is usually the House Manager's job to have direct dealings with them, to order the supplies they need and to acquiesce in the particular, if sometimes apparently eccentric, preferences they may express for some products or tools as against others (even though he may himself have other preferences). He must ensure that a room in the theatre, however small, is set aside and adequately furnished for the all-important tea-breaks. Without the cleaners' liking and co-operation, he will be totally unable to achieve the desired object of having a thoroughly spruce and attractive building of which the cared-for look will not escape the eye of the patrons. This effect may never be commented on if it is fully achieved, but any deficiency will be noted.

*In toto*, the Assistant Manager is responsible primarily for the physical impression of the building and for making all who use it, including the audience, take a pride in it. The day-to-day details may seem humdrum, but nothing is more off-putting than a sullen reception, or no reception at all, bad service, and dust in the corners! It is by no means a dead-end routine. A House Manager worth his salt will be quick to spot things which can be improved, whether it be an extra space for a small new bar, a new design for crockery, or guiding an architect in the planning of the audience's perambulations round the front of house territory in a project for a new building. To make the best of his job he needs to be observant, pleasant, and above all to care about people, whether they are the paying public or the theatre staff.

# 19

## *THE ADMINISTRATOR*
## *AS LICENSEE*

The Administrator holds in his personal capacity a number of licences from various bodies and authorities, which define his legal responsibilities to these bodies and of which the terms must at all times be strictly observed. Everyone must have noticed at some time the notices which proclaim the right to sell beers, wines and spirits on the premises, and state that a building is licensed for music, singing and dancing. These are only two of the statements behind which lie a network of injunctions and regulations.

For practical purposes, they can be divided into four sections—

I. Relating to the actual building and devised for the safety of the public during the conduct of performances.

II. Relating to licensed bars and other facilities.

III. Defining the entertainments which can be exhibited on the premises and the times when these may take place.

IV. Governing the use of special devices on the stage and matters concerning the actual productions.

The Administrator has multifarious responsibilities in all these categories and many of the rules apply whether the theatre activity is amateur or professional. The penalties for transgression are severe and it is essential for special permissions to be applied for well before the opening date of productions. A little research into what is required may save a great deal of trouble since in these as in other legal matters ignorance of the law is no plea for defence.

### I. THE THEATRE LICENCE

Every theatre and cinema holds a licence from the local authority.

This licence is a vitally important document which lays down the conditions of licensing the building for performances in detailed requirements, both for the building, its structure and conduct, and for the physical presentation of the plays. These rules are legally binding on the licensee and he is personally responsible for seeing that they are carried out either by him or by an accredited deputy. They are basically devised for the safety of the audience both on normal occasions of performance and in the dreaded emergency of panic caused by fire. No manager under-rates their importance or would knowingly infringe these regulations.

The conditions of the licence vary from city to city but the general nature of the responsibility is summed up in some statement such as this quoted from the Oxford City licence—

The licensee or the person nominated by him shall take all due precautions for the safety of the public, the performers and employees and shall retain control over all portions of the premises.

The requirements for the front of house include the following—

*Attendants.* Number required in proportion to the number of seats. Distinctive dress.

*Exits.* All exits to be marked as such and to be practical during performance and thrown open at the end. All parts of the premises open to the public to be clear of obstruction. Ways out to be indicated.

*Parking.* Not to interfere with the free use of exits or to be within a certain distance of such exits.

*Furnishings.* Secure floor covering and no risk of obstruction. Curtains not to be hung across gangways or staircases. If across exits, to draw easily and hang clear of the floor. All permanent decoration to be fireproof.

*General lighting.* Public areas and ways out to have electric light. If there should be a failure the audience must leave after one hour unless the general supply is restored.

*Secondary lighting.* Electricity supplied by a source other than that of the general lighting is to be used for auditorium, ways out and notices indicating ways out. If this secondary system fails the audience must leave immediately.

*Fire precautions.* Extinguishers to be kept in allotted positions and tested regularly. The licensee and at least two other members of his staff must know how to use fire-fighting appliances and the front-of-house and backstage staff must all be instructed in the procedure for dealing with an outbreak until the arrival of the fire-brigade. Regular fire-drills to be held.

*Safety curtain.* This is a specific requirement which may be insisted on by the local Fire Authorities under certain conditions issued by the Home Office. In the case of thrust and open stages it may be impossible to install a safety curtain, in which case it may be necessary to comply with special instructions issued by the licensing authority.

The object of the safety curtain is to seal off the stage in the event of fire and to prevent escape of smoke into the auditorium, which has been found from past experience to be the most likely cause of panic. The safety curtain has a quick-release mechanism which can be operated either from the stage door, or in the prompt corner by the Stage Manager. This must be tested periodically. Also, it is the responsibility of the House Manager to ensure that the safety curtain is raised and lowered at least once during each performance. It is of vital importance that the safety curtain is down before the theatre is left after the evening performance. A fire, perhaps started in the auditorium by a carelessly discarded cigarette, could probably be confined to the auditorium and avoid an expensive total loss. Such loss has been caused by neglect of this precaution and although the fire would probably cause the eventual fall of the safety curtain, the evidence of neglect will be evident to the expert.

In conjunction with the safety curtain there must also be over the stage a lantern light with a fusible link which allows windows to fall open to draw smoke and flame upwards and to relieve pressure.

*Fireproofing on stage.* The risk of fire is the danger most dreaded in theatres and cinemas. It is a regulation that materials used on the stage must be non-flam, including costumes. The British Standards Institution, 2 Park Street, London, W.1., publishes a handy pamphlet, called *Performance Requirements of Materials for Flameproof Clothing.* Materials must be tested for their fireproof qualities, and some are forbidden, such as polythene, cotton-wool, etc., and anything which may flare.

The Greater London Council has issued a booklet *Play Safe* invaluable for those companies using a building without full stage facilities for theatrical performances. It is a guide to the precautions considered necessary at public performances in, say, multi-purpose halls and open stages. At 3s. it is very good value.

### II. LICENCES FOR THEATRE FACILITIES (OTHER THAN THE PLAY)

The Administrator is also the equivalent of a publican since the bars and restaurants in theatre premises come within the province of the Customs and Excise regulations for the sale of beers, wines, spirits and cigarettes. The terms of the licence vary according to local licensing regulations, but in general the ruling is that such sales are for the theatre audience only and are restricted to the times when the public are on the premises for performances. If a restaurant, as distinct from theatre bars, is on the premises and is open at other times of the day, additional rules apply both to the sale of liquor and, under the Catering Wages Act, to staff pay and hours of work.

Nowadays, when theatres aim to offer greatly increased facilities, these may include the sale of books, magazines, musical scores, records, etc., related to the productions. This is very laudable, but care must be taken that there is no infringement of agreements with local book-sellers and record shops, and the theatre may even have to become, by agreement with the Local Chamber of Commerce, a member of the recognized trade associations.

### III. LICENCES RELATING TO THE PRODUCTIONS AND THEIR TIMES OF SHOWING

#### 1. THE THEATRES ACT, 1968
September 27th 1968 became an historic date in the history

of the British theatre, because on that day the censorship exercised by the Lord Chamberlain over the presentation of stage plays became obsolete. In June 1967 the proceedings of the Joint Committee on Censorship of the Theatre, with the Minutes of Evidence, were made public, and remain an interesting and exhaustive document giving the history of the office and powers of the Lord Chamberlain in the theatre, and the views of practising dramatists and theatre managers of today. Its general conclusion sums up the ensuing change in legislation.

"The anachronistic licensing powers of the Lord Chamberlain will be abolished and will not be replaced by any other form of pre-censorship, national or local. The theatre will be subjected to the general law of the land, and those presenting plays which break the law will be subjected to prosecution under the relevant procedure . . . Political censorship of any kind will cease."

The Theatres Act, 1968 repeals the Theatres Act, 1843.

A change so revolutionary requires careful study by those upon whom the responsibility now falls, and anyone concerned with the presentation of stage plays should study the Theatres Act in detail. A useful starting point is provided by the Home Office Memorandum for Theatre Interests, bearing in mind the injunction with which it is prefaced, that "if there is any doubt on a particular point legal advice should be sought."

The main points may be summarized as follows—

### (i) *Obscene Performances*

It is a criminal act to *present* or *direct* an obscene performance of a play in public or in private. The latter term includes *club performances*.

### (ii) *Specific Provision*

Prosecution may be undertaken for any of the following—

(*a*) *Obscenity*. This is defined as the tendency of the performance taken as a whole to deprave or corrupt persons who will be likely to attend it.

(*b*) *Incitement to racial hatred.* A person who presents or directs a play involving the use of threatening, abusive or insulting words is guilty of an offence if he did so with intent to stir up racial hatred *and* if the performance taken as a whole is likely to stir up such hatred.

(*c*) *Breach of the peace.* As for (*b*) if the intent is to provoke a breach of the peace or if the performance as a whole is likely to do so.

(*d*) *Sedition.* Acts, words or writings intended or calculated to disturb the tranquillity of the State by creating disaffection towards the person of the Sovereign or in various other ways.

(*e*) *Libel.* The publication of "words" in the performance of a play will be grounds for proceedings for libel rather than slander. "Words" are defined to include "pictures, visual images, gestures and other methods of signifying meaning."

## (iii) *Definition of a Play*

All kinds of performances, *public or private* except the following—

Domestic occasions in a private dwelling;
Rehearsal or performance given solely or primarily for making a record;
Film or radio or television broadcast.

## (iv) *Liability for Prosecution*

(*a*) Liability falls on *the person or persons who presented or directed* an obscene performance. A person may be held to have directed a performance even if he was not present at it.

(*b*) *An actor* is to be treated as if he were the director of the performance if, without reasonable excuse, he acts otherwise than in accordance with the director's directions.

(*c*) *The licensee* of a theatre, as such, is *not* liable, unless, exceptionally, he presents or directs a play or is so closely connected with it as to be liable under the general law relating to aiding and abetting.

(*d*) *A body corporate* may be held to have committed an offence with the consent or connivance of, or through the neglect of, any director, manager, secretary or similar officer.

These individuals may be proceeded against as well as the body corporate.

## (v) *Enforcement*

(*a*) In England and Wales, proceedings may not be taken without the consent of the Attorney General.

(*b*) The script, i.e. the working text, together with stage and other directions is admissible evidence, rather than the standard published edition of the play.

(*c*) The police have powers to obtain a copy of the script.

(*d*) The police have the necessary powers of entry and inspection, as have also, where appropriate, the officers of the licensing authority.

## (vi) *Deposit of Scripts*

It is obligatory for a copy of the script on which the public performance of any *new* play is based to be delivered to the Trustees of the British Museum free of charge within one month of the performance. Scripts should be sent to the Keeper of Manuscripts, British Museum, Bloomsbury, W.C.1. "New" plays is defined so as to make the requirement apply only to scripts of the first night performance, and to exclude other performances based on substantially the same script and performances based on a text already published in the United Kingdom, which would be already subject to the requirement to deposit under the Copyright Act 1911 (s.11).

## (vii) *Licensing*

(*a*) *Extension of licensing.* Because of the wide definition of the word "play," premises in which a public performance is given which may involve, say, singing, dancing and sketches, will now require a theatre licence as well as the music and dancing licence formerly needed.

(*b*) *Licensing Authority.* The new licensing system is substantially the same as under the 1843 Act, except that the Greater London Council is now the licensing authority for premises used as theatres in the Greater London Area, and there may be variations in the procedure of some local authorities.

The authority of the licensing body is not now extended to conditions about the nature of plays which may be performed, but is still concerned with regulations about physical safety and health.

Notice of intention to sell intoxicating liquor on the premises must still be given to the Clerk of the licensing justices.

It is still too soon to observe the full effects of the new latitude, but the Lord Chamberlain's power was for so long a thorn in the flesh of dramatists and managers that the change cannot but be finally beneficial.

## 2. THE AUTHOR'S OR AGENT'S LICENCE TO PERFORM A PLAY

### (a) Copyright

The necessary permission to perform a play by a living author or authors dead for less than fifty years or first published within the last fifty years but after the death of the author is bound up with the laws of copyright and the payment of royalties for stage productions either to the author or to those who handle his estate. These matters are most usually dealt with by an accredited literary agent or through a society such as the Society of Authors. It is essential for permission to perform a play to have been obtained well before public announcements of the performance are made. This is another of the legal responsibilities of the Administrator who will be held personally responsible for any breach of copyright.

### (b) Content of the Play

It is not always realized that, should proceedings be threatened for any libel thought to be contained in a play, the Administrator, in his capacity as Licensee of the theatre presenting the play, is legally culpable. While action is pending an injunction may be taken out against him if he does not immediately withdraw the play from further performances.

It is the contract between the author and the Administrator which offers protection against such situations as it includes the author's warranty that the play contains no defamatory

matter. Even this, however, cannot protect the Licensee of
the theatre should action be threatened or taken.

### (c) Royalties

A certain percentage of the gross box-office takings is normally
paid to the agent for distribution to the author. This is subject to negotiation, but for general purposes may be said to
vary in the region of five to ten per cent. There are a few
authors, notably George Bernard Shaw (who is represented,
incidentally, by the Society of Authors) for whom special and
inflexible royalty rates are laid down.

Other factors taken into account when royalty rates are
calculated are the seating capacity of the theatre, since a normal
percentage in a very small theatre might represent an unrea-
sonably high sum in relation both to the total Box Office take
and to the financial scope of the management; the situation
of the theatre, since a provincial theatre may *ipso facto* have a
reasonably smaller expectation of high box-office receipts;
and the distinction between amateur and professional status
of the management presenting the play. Amateurs should note,
too, that they may be able to pay *pro rata* per performance.
This can be of great benefit in calculating the total budget for
the production.

### 3. THEATRE OPENING TIMES

#### Normal Provisions

The Theatre Licence granted by the Justices usually states
that public performances may be given on weekdays only.
Theatres are not usually allowed to open for this purpose on
Sundays, Christmas Day, Good Friday or "days appointed
for public fast and thanksgiving." There are naturally variations in some localities, as, for instance, in the North of England,
where performances may be given on Good Friday.

A nightly time of closure, usually before midnight, is also
stipulated in the licence.

#### Sunday Performances

The general opening of theatres for public performances on
Sundays is at present forbidden.

This may change in the future if recommendations in the Crathorne Report[1] are followed by Governmental proposals to amend the legislation currently in force.

The Lord's Day Observance Society can make representations to the police and the local authority if they object to public entertainment on Sunday, and the police may, if they agree with such representation, cause the performance in question to be cancelled.

The implications of Sunday opening for the theatrical profession are not quite as straightforward as they may appear at first sight. All artists are entitled to a six-day working week and Sunday opening would mean giving a free day during the week without a performance. This might well be met by closing, say, on Monday, notoriously one of the least profitable days. It would be a matter of training the public to a new habit and the ingrained puritanical English attitude towards Sunday would have to give place to the continental attitude which takes the theatre as Sunday entertainment as a matter of course. It is undoubtedly an anomaly that cinemas may open at a stated time in the afternoon or evening, frequently to show the less reputable films for an audience which is glad to accept anything as a relief from tedium. Financially there would be problems which would have to be solved with the introduction of new rulings—the payment of over-time rates to staff on Sundays being one of them.

Otherwise there is little doubt that freedom to count Sunday as a day of performance would give greater flexibility to the programming of plays, especially when repertoire is being operated. The famous English weekend habit may die hard, but it is possible that there might be advantages in giving artists a free weekday instead of Sunday. Members of the profession are at present unable to see performances by other companies, except when matinées of their own do not coincide. Busman's holiday though this may appear to be, actors are always curious about their colleagues' activities and it can be of great advantage to the young actor particularly to see as many productions as possible. A rota system of days of closure

---

[1] *Report of the Departmental Committee on the Law on Sunday Observance* (published 1964). This report is a mine of information about the present legal situation and the move towards a change.

could perhaps be devised for the West End theatre, and a similar plan for other towns which have more than one theatre. These and all the many questions raised by a new ruling are already being fully discussed by managers.

This state of affairs is, however, still conjectural and in the future. There are at present particular instances in which Sunday performances may be given, with special conditions—

(*a*) "*Public dancing, singing and music* or other public entertainment of the like kind" are allowed on Sundays, under the conditions of the Sunday Entertainment Act, 1932. A licence to open for this purpose is granted by the local Justices and is in addition to the Theatre Licence. The opening and closing times are stipulated and the conditions are similar to those of the general Licence, including the presence during such performances of the Licensee or a nominee.

This licence permits a theatre to hold concerts, recitals, poetry readings, etc., which do not involve the use of make-up and costume. The public may buy tickets in the ordinary way and the entertainment may be publicly advertised.

(*b*) *Club Performances.* Theatres which are run as clubs for members only include the Arts Theatre in London and some provincial theatres, such as the Leatherhead Theatre and the Castle Theatre at Farnham. Membership is by payment of a fixed annual subscription and this entitles members only to buy tickets, usually on production of the membership card at the Box Office. The buying of drinks on the premises is restricted to members. A bona-fide club, attached to a theatre but having a separate constitution and limited to those members who pay a subscription, may hold performances in the building on Sundays for members and their guests only. In general, the following procedure applies—

*Publicity* for a club performance. The performance may be advertised only to members of the organization, i.e. by letter or circular and not advertised publicly in any way which may give the impression that it is open to the general public. All such announcements should include clearly the proviso that it is for members and their guests only.

I. *Billingham Forum*

II. *Collegiate Theatre, University College, London*

III. *Stage and Auditorium, Octagon Theatre, Bolton*

IV. *The Foyer, Nottingham Playhc*

V. *Exhibition Courtyard, Basildon Arts Centre*

VI. *Model of the New National Theatre, South Bank, London*

VII. *Exterior, Chichester Festival Theatre*

VIII. *New Restaurant (1968), Liverpool Playhouse*

*Tickets* for a club performance may be on sale at the box office, but may be sold only to members who must produce evidence of membership when they purchase their tickets. No ticket may be sold to a member of the general public. Some theatres find it useful to sell numbered programmes for such events. This can be of assistance with the staff problems which may be encountered on Sundays.

### IV. SPECIAL LICENCES APPERTAINING TO THE PRODUCTIONS

#### 1. MUSIC

##### (i) *The Use of Music during the Intervals and During the Action of the Play*

The Performing Right Society Limited is described as "An Association of Composers, Authors and Publishers of Music." It owns the performing right in music and lyrics composed or written by its members.

All theatres which in the course of their programme may include variety shows, musical shows or musical revues, concert party entertainment and pantomimes, hold a licence from the Society. For this a royalty is paid in advance at the beginning of the licence year. This is on account of performing rights or royalties related to the specific performances for which these payments have to be made. The actual amounts payable are assessed according to a tariff agreed by the Theatres National Committee and the Music Users' Council, taking into account the location of the theatre (London or provincial) and its seating capacity.

The Licensee must furnish detailed returns of music to which these payments apply. Lists are not supplied because, as the Society states in its leaflet NC, any list would quickly become out of date and would be bulky and expensive and difficult to use. This leaflet further states—

The Society has been established in the interests of those concerned in the public performance of music no less than in that of copyright owners, to convey by one licence the right to perform an enormous variety of British and foreign works, thus avoiding the necessity of making direct application to the owner of the performing right in each separate work.

*Definition of Copyright.* The Performing Right Society Pamphlet H defines very clearly the right, under the Copyright Act, 1956, as "the sole right of performing or authorizing the performance of the work in public." This right lasts "for the life of the composer or author and fifty years thereafter." The moneys due in return for the permission are paid to the composers or authors, or to the family or representatives of those no longer living. The payment for the use of music in the action of a play is required of amateurs as well as professionals.

There are distinctions between "curtain" and "incidental" music, musical plays and operas, musical entertainments, including concerts and Sunday shows. These are all clearly set out in the leaflet *Music in Theatres* issued by the Performing Right Society, which repays study on these points. All points of detail and other queries are dealt with by The Performing Right Society, Licensing Department, 29/33 Berners Street, London, W.1 (Telephone 01–580–5544, Extension 36).

## (ii) *Licence for the Use of Recorded Music*

This licence is granted by Phonographic Performance Limited. It governs the use of recorded music used in the course of productions in intervals and for play-in and play-out music. In connection with the licence, for which a fee is payable in advance, accurate returns must periodically be submitted to the company of all recorded music so used.

It is intended that this shall not only check on the fees due for copyright performances but shall also protect the interests of live musicians. Theatres are not thereby allowed to substitute recorded music if musicians are regularly employed or where, an orchestra pit being part of the building, a live orchestra could be employed. There are in fact very few modern theatres which have a permanent orchestra pit or employ an orchestra, as was usual in some of the large nineteenth century touring theatres. Equally, the use of music as a part of the production, where it is not so much "incidental" as an integral part of the production, is now much more common.

## 2. SPECIAL EFFECTS ON STAGE

### (i) *Fire-arms*

The Licensee of a theatre usually holds a fire-arms certificate, which has to be produced, with the appropriate variation granted by the police when a fire-arm is used on the stage during the action of a play. Firms which hire such weapons will not issue them unless the certificate is produced.

The "variation" for each occasion is obtained by filling in a form obtainable from the local police station with exact details of the fire-arms requested and the number of blank cartridges required. The fee of 2s. 6d. per variation certificate is required. The form is countersigned by or on behalf of the Chief Constable of the area and is inserted into the Fire-arm Certificate book.

Naturally great care has to be taken that weapons which might be a danger are locked away when not in use. It is best to detail the Stage Manager or a responsible member of the stage staff to make it his special charge. The fire-arms should be kept in a lockable cupboard or safe, taken out just before the performance, retrieved from the actor or from the stage-manager after use and locked up again immediately. It is well-known that the police are most anxious that such weapons should not fall into the hands of unauthorized persons, and the Licensee of the theatre is responsible for seeing that this does not happen.

### (ii) *Naked Lights*

This is part of the stringent precautions against the dreaded catastrophe of a theatre—fire. It has already been stated that all materials used on the stage must be non-flammable, but in addition, special written permission must be sought from the police and fire-authorities for the use of naked lights on the stage. These may be in the form of candles or candelabras, especially in period plays, or the flaming torches which have illuminated many a stirring scene in productions of Shakespeare.

Written application should be made to the police stating the number of candles to be used, where they are lit (i.e. on or off stage), by whom they are carried during the action, how long they remain alight, and where exactly in the action of the play they are used, i.e. the act and scene. The more detail that can be given the better.

Permission may be given with firm conditions, e.g. that the naked flame is kept well clear of draperies and costumes, that it is extinguished the moment it is brought off-stage, that an extra fire-extinguisher is placed beside the stage near the point where the flame is used. Note also (all ye directors who have bright ideas at the last minute!) there is usually a stipulated time within which such applications must be made *before* the opening of the production. The police and fire-officers may wish to watch rehearsals to assure themselves that there is no danger.

Cigarettes lit in the course of the action are usually allowed, but the stage-management must see that there is an adequate number of ash-trays on the set.

The flaming torches must be constructed to burn for a limited time only, and a "cold" flame (i.e. from a methylated spirit formula) must be used.

### (iii) *Fireworks and Electrically-detonated Explosions*

As for naked lights, detailed applications for the use of these effects must be sent to the police. Fireworks of certain kinds (e.g. sparklers) may be more readily allowed than more explosive kinds. The author had once to appear before the City Magistrates to ask for the use of a "threepenny banger" in a play! This was allowed, but with strict precautions about fire-extinguishers, and the stipulation that it had to be aimed up-stage, well away from the audience.

Electrically detonated explosions, if allowed, must be under the supervision of experienced and responsible stage-staff. Efficient devices can be obtained, with advice on how to use them, from the Strand Electric and Engineering Company. The amateur concoction of such explosive devices is firmly to be discouraged!

### 3. LICENCE FOR THE EMPLOYMENT OF CHILDREN IN STAGE ENTERTAINMENT

In October 1968 new regulations were brought into force laying down detailed conditions for children taking part in all kinds of performances, including, for the first time, television. Part II of the Children and Young Persons Act 1963 and the Children (Performances) Regulations 1968 came into full operation on 3rd March, 1969. The Act and the Regulations should be read together and the Home Office booklet *The Law on Performances by Children*, H.M.S.O. 1968, provides an invaluable guide to their provisions.

Some salient points are as follows—

1. *Age.* A child aged 13 and under compulsory school age must in general be licensed for stage performances by the local authority. There are exceptions for children under 13 in some opera and ballet performances and special acting parts.

2. *Rehearsals.* Time spent rehearsing may in some cases be counted towards the total permitted performing time.

3. *Education.* Absence from school may be authorized but the child's education is safeguarded by certain conditions and restrictions. Arrangements must be carefully checked with the local authority unless performances are during school holidays.

4. *Matron.* A person approved by the licensing authority must accompany the child throughout the period of the engagement, except when he is in the charge of his parent or teacher.

5. *Period of Performance.* The regulations state that a child of 13 or over may only be employed for a period of 80 days in a twelve-month period, and a child under 13 for 40 days during a similar period. The number of hours spent performing and rehearsing every week is limited. There are specific conditions about all aspects of the child's health, welfare and education and the many arrangements which affect these. All managers should be thoroughly conversant with the far-reaching provisions of the Act and Regulations to which the Home Office Guide draws attention.

TAKING CHILDREN ABROAD WITH PLAYS

Licences for children to take part in performances outside the United Kingdom and the Irish Republic are granted by the

Chief Magistrate at Bow Street, London, W.C.2. The Chief Constable of the district in which the child lives must be given at least seven days notice of the intended application, and must see the contract of employment. The Chief Magistrate may impose any restrictions or conditions which he thinks fit.

# 20

# THEATRE CONTROL

THE Theatre Licence is not a piece of paper which can be put away in a drawer and conveniently forgotten. It enforces actual inspection and the front-of-house staff are as busy as backstage preparing for the performance.

There are few consecutive hours in the day of the administrative staff of the theatre which can be described as regular and invariable but this preparation is one exception. For these hours a routine must be established for the members of the staff concerned so that all the essential procedures can be regularly performed and checked. These procedures relate in the main to the terms of the Theatre Licence for safety and to the public bars and other facilities. The person responsible for opening the premises is by the terms of this licence, the licensee or his nominated representative. If in fact he delegates this duty to his assistant or the House Manager, as is usual, both must understand that the licensee is finally responsible.

Obviously there are variations in each theatre, but the general lines are as follows (for general purposes it is assumed that these duties fall by agreement to the House Manager).

### BEFORE THE PERFORMANCE

#### 1. *General Inspection*

About an hour before the performance, the House Manager should go over the entire area of the theatre used by the public. He may be accompanied by the fireman if the theatre is required to have one on its strength by the requirements of the local licensing authority. He must see for himself that all exits are unlocked and that the doors open easily and correctly. All curtains across doors must be drawn aside according to specifications so that they cause no obstruction.

All the lighting fixtures and the secondary lighting must be put on to ensure that no bulbs have failed. Even though a regular check on bulbs (called "the lamp-round") will be conducted as a matter of course by the theatre electricians, bulbs can fail at any moment and must be replaced before the audience arrives.

There must be no obstruction in any passage or gangway, no carpet ruckled up or working loose.

Rehearsing companies should leave the auditorium tidy but sometimes personal property is left behind and cigarette ends overlooked; all these have to be tidied away.

Car-parking is usually prohibited round theatres to allow for a panic exit by the audience and for fire-engines to approach the building. This must be checked nightly.

### 2. *Staff Preparations*

The usherettes or helpers responsible for the sale of programmes must all be assembled and given their floats. Casual staff must have an eagle, if benign, eye kept on their punctuality. Coming as they often do from other jobs, they have difficulties but should be impressed with the need for being in their overalls (the "distinctive dress" usually required by the licence) and spruced up well before the "half" when the public are admitted. Time should be allowed for each helper to check the float and her issue of programmes so that there are no recriminations later.

The bar should be laid out and stock issued and checked at a stipulated time before the public is admitted to the premises. The House Manager must cast an eye over all the areas, making sure that all is in order and that staff are present. If the absence of a member of staff passes unnoticed by any unfortunate chance, chaos may ensue.

The usherettes must then be deployed in the auditorium (cajoled into not congregating into little groups) ready to show the public to their seats.

### 3. *The Half*

Only when he is satisfied that all the premises and staff are in order and ready can the House Manager give the signal for the public to be admitted, half an hour before the starting time. He himself should then be in the foyer, looking, we hope, relaxed and cheerful, but watchful none the less for any incipient problems and, more pleasant duty, quick to greet friends of the theatre, regular patrons or anyone who needs special attention.

### 4. *The Start of the Performance*

Many small theatres, particularly those run on comparatively personal lines in the provinces, require the stage management to await a signal from the front of house before starting the performance. This can be extremely useful if there is a sudden influx to the box office in the last few minutes. If the stage management start regardless, the first moments of the play are ruined for the punctual members of the audience by the tramp of late-comers' feet and jostling into seats.

There is a knotty problem here. The start of the performance should be unfailingly punctual. To start late is demoralizing for the actors, bad for those who have only a narrow margin to catch the last bus at the end, and encourages late-coming ("oh, they never start on time"), and so the rot sets in.

Unfortunately, very few theatres have the facilities for dealing with late-comers—either a specially isolated space at the back of the theatre or an adjoining room with closed-circuit television—where they can be kept until the earliest suitable pause when they may be let into the auditorium. Some managements put up a notice to the effect that late-comers will be excluded until the earliest suitable pause. This can make for some very unhappy moments when the House Manager meets the occasional customer who says he has paid for his seat and insists on taking it, creating a disturbance if he is in any way deterred. Not all plays have a convenient break near the beginning. All one can say is that if a management takes a stand it must be consistent in enforcing the directive, so that the practice is well-known and may gradually be better obeyed. But this is a situation which calls for all the tact, charm, firmness and persuasion which are a House Manager's stock in trade.

One point which can be helpful. The muttered, infuriating conversations and clinking of cash for the sale of programmes to late-comers in the dark can be eliminated by putting a programme-seller outside the auditorium (if programmes are not already on sale in the foyer) so that late-comers can at least spend their enforced delay in reading the cast list before they go in.

## DURING THE PERFORMANCE

The House Manager must resign himself to restless evenings while he is on duty during performances. There can be no tranquil watching of the play for him.

When all the late-comers have been safely stowed, he should make a rapid tour of the front-of-house area and the bars. A quick tidy-up in the cloakrooms, on the stairs, in the foyer, etc., makes all the difference to the look of the building when the audience emerges for the interval. He should see that all the bars, coffee and sweet counters, etc., are being tidied up and re-stacked ready for the next bout, and that there are no members of the public other than theatre-ticket-holders at large on the premises, unless they are visiting an open exhibition area or the restaurant perhaps. He will receive the box-office money for safe-keeping, the nightly returns, and the used ticket-books, all of which have to be checked.

## THE INTERVAL

Towards the end of the act before the interval, a warning bell from the stage (a low buzz, please, not one that peals throughout the whole building) warns him that the coffee service, ice-cream sellers, etc., should be ready for action.

He and other responsible staff should be at their allotted posts to pull aside curtains, open doors, etc. A check must be made of the lowering of the safety curtain which is statutorily required to be done in the presence of the audience.

During the interval theatre staff should keep a look-out in the licensed bars to see that no young people under age are in these areas, let alone being served in the crush by a bar-staff sometimes too rushed to notice the customers.

The House Manager should be seen to be available during the interval to sort out any problems, queries or complaints.

The warning bells for the end of the interval warn not only the audience that they should return but the theatre staff that they must pull curtains, close doors, check cloakrooms and return thereafter to the final clearing-up.

### AFTER THE INTERVAL

When the performance is under way after the last interval, the House Manager will in his office receive and check the money and returns for all the saleable commodities disposed of during the evening. If time allows (it sometimes does not, if the last act of the play is only, say, thirty-five or forty minutes) he should check as much as possible on the spot, since mistakes are easier to trace at once. If the time is too short, it is a good idea to place the cash and papers in sealed envelopes for checking and banking the following morning.

### AFTER THE PERFORMANCE

The warning bell for the end of the performance means Action Stations again for the staff, doors and curtains manned for the audience departure, then a quick tour of the auditorium for lost property and to the final locking up round and inspection to leave the theatre empty and secure for the night. Departure may well be delayed on this score by the chivvying of actors who like to dally for a gossip after the show, but finally all must be cleared before the House Manager can leave with a peaceful mind (unless the final check is delegated to the fireman or night watchman).

A final warning—a careful check must be made all over the theatre for smouldering cigarette ends and for gas-rings, electric-fires, irons, etc., left on, and any other fire hazard.

# 21

# PUBLICITY AND PUBLIC RELATIONS

THESE two areas of theatre work are linked here because they overlap, the purpose of both being to establish the theatre in its local community and continuously to increase the audience. In many theatres the work is done by one person, but in the last year or two many small and regional theatres have used some of their increased Arts Council grant to separate them and to appoint a Public Relations Officer whose full-time job is to build audiences. There is some overlapping, but the territories of the work can be generally defined.

## PUBLICITY

### PRINTING AND DESIGN

The theatre has been comparatively slow to learn from the tremendous strides made by industry in presentation and packaging. Posters of an old-fashioned design crammed with information so detailed that it defeats its own ends are at last beginning to give way to more "with it" typography, design and colour. Better still is the recognition of the impact on the public of having a consistent design plan linking all printed matter issued from the theatre—posters, hanging cards, programmes, throwaways and even the writing paper used by management and Box Office. Some of this progress is due to the pioneering of the big subsidized companies, such as the Royal Shakespeare, the National Theatre and Sadler's Wells. Presenting plays over a long period, they have weighed up the methods by which the public may immediately recognize a characteristic design, which can be varied while retaining the essential character to indicate a new phase of productions and booking periods.

A further contribution to the increasing clarity of typographical design is the breaking-down of the star system, which could frequently cause a poster to be unpleasingly crowded with names in huge type. This is now frequently replaced by the democratically alphabetical list of the company. Naturally a theatre normally using a resident company needs to make much of the special appearance of a star from time to time, but this event is more startlingly apparent when such names appear on a format normally uncluttered.

Each theatre must judge for itself the design most likely to appeal to its audience, but there are a few principles which appear to be of general use—

### 1. *Design*

It is worth paying a fee to a professional typographer and/or designer to obtain a striking and artistically pleasing result. Competition is now so great, advertising is so high-powered and extensive, and the general standard set by industry and the retail trades is so high that anything mediocre is swamped on the hoardings or in the piles of circulars which arrive on every breakfast table.

### 2. *Colour*

Research has shown that there are certain colour combinations which are psychologically very effective and account could well be taken of this factor.

Theatres customarily use regularly rented sites for their posters on the assumption that there may be a number of people living there or passing daily who will use it for reference. Changes of colour, perhaps with the retention of basic design to keep continuity, can make a fresh impact from time to time.

### MATERIAL AND METHOD

### 1. *Posters*

Most theatres print specific numbers of posters which are posted on the same sites by the local bill-poster. It should be part of the Publicity Manager's job to go round regularly to check that the bill-posting is being done punctually. Even the best-regulated firms can lapse. He should also make himself aware of changes in the locality. It is no use going on having posters printed for sites that are becoming derelict or may even have ceased to exist in the rapidly-changing world of town-planning. In fact, he must personally acquaint himself with the effectiveness of all the sites, and look for new ones as housing estates spread.

## 2. *Hanging Cards*
These may or may not still be a useful means of advertising. As more and more super-markets and self-service combines replace the friendly little shop, it is probably questionable whether the hanging card still serves its purpose. Noticeboards in libraries and other public meeting-places are covered with such literature. There may be people who look regularly for theatre information in such places, but the theatre's cards, unless very striking, are liable to be overlooked.

## 3. *Handwritten Sheets*
When displayed on large hoardings these hit the eye—they may even be eyesores by some standards—but they make an impression. The Publicity Manager should also examine these sites regularly and increase or diminish the number used according to the locale.

## 4. *The Mailing List*
It is usually regarded as the main spring of publicity, since it reaches individuals while posters, hanging-cards, etc., may be wasting their information on the unregarding passer-by. A few special hints may be useful on maintaining the forcefulness of the brochure and its distribution.

(i) *Method.* One of the various addressing card systems may be used. Envelopes can be put through a machine with great speed as compared with the use of a separate card index. The cards are durable and can be prepared by a secretary in the theatre. They are obtainable in different colours, which may indicate different categories, e.g. adjoining counties, schools, party bookings, theatre club members, etc. New variations on this system are always being evolved and it is worth keeping up-to-date with methods used for bulk addressing by industrial firms. The days of slave labour for the addressing of envelopes are past, thank goodness. Computer tape is now used by some organizations, including the Royal Opera House, Covent Garden.

(ii) *Bringing the Mailing List up to Date.* Beware of theatres which boast of a mailing list of several thousands! There are notable exceptions, like the National and Royal Shakespeare Theatres, but in general, mailing lists contain a lot of dead wood on which printing and postage costs are lavished to no avail.

The list should be revised at least annually. This can be done with a business-reply envelope, or by the system of enclosing with an issue of the whole list a card of confirmation to be returned by a specified date. The National Theatre has a good system of using the actual marked card for mailing list purposes. It pays to be ruthless and remove the cards for those who have not thus replied. The interested people soon notice that they have not received the next issue and repair their fault of omission. In this way one can be as sure as is humanly possible that all who receive the list are likely to come to the theatre at some time, which is the most one can hope for.

(iii) *Postage Charge.* Most theatres in these days of high and ever-rising postal charges have an annual charge to help cover the cost of sending regular advance booking information. This varies from 2s. 6d. to 10s. and it is up to each management to gauge how far it can go. While all are anxious to disseminate information about the programme as widely as possible, a charge can act as a salutary deterrent for collectors only. Ideally perhaps the service should be free, but few theatres could afford this.

(iv) *Information from the Mailing List.* Each address should of course be absolutely accurate, and it is not so unnecessary as it may appear to stress this point. It is surprising how many people either leave out, say, the county, or write so badly that the address may be wrongly copied.

There should be on each card the date of accession, so that no one is asked a second time for a subscription recently paid. This particular hazard is avoided by making all renewed subscriptions valid from January 1st, though one still has then to deal with those who join much later in the year.

An accurate and well-maintained mailing list can be used in many ways and is statistical material for general information about the audience. The Publicity Manager and the Public Relations Officer may find it helpful to know how many there are from various areas. If some parts of the locality seem not to be adequately represented, it may help to take more newspaper space in local papers there, find poster sites, or open an agency.

(v) *Party Bookings.* This is an increasing and lucrative activity in many theatres. A separate section of the mailing list should be built up, if possible in conjunction with a record of performances attended and tickets booked. Coach firms and private hire firms are a useful source for party bookings as well as the obvious societies, theatre supporters clubs, youth clubs, conferences, Rotarians, amateur dramatic societies, etc. The Arts Council Transport Subsidy is a great inducement to regular party bookings. (This scheme is fully explained in the section on the Arts Council and other bodies connected with the theatre, page 59.)

(vi) *Pro-formas.* When people write in for a brochure it is useful to return with it a pro-forma explaining that the list will be sent regularly if requested by the return of the form duly filled up with the details, plus the subscription if required. A pro-forma for obtaining the Arts Council Transport subsidy for party bookings is also helpful for the party organizer and is a book-keeping check for the theatre.

(vii) *Newspaper Advertisements.* The regular advertisement in daily local papers is obviously a useful investment. It can be costly and should be kept to the minimum, giving names of actors and other personnel only when the management considers this to be a box-office draw. It should always give clearly the theatre's address and telephone, hours of booking times and prices. Considerable trial and error is involved until the Publicity Manager finds out which are the most popular papers. Even then, there will always be protests from patrons in outlying hamlets without a paper which caters for them. This advertising is not cheap, and unless the budget is very large the advertising has to be selective. Regional theatres have a special section in the *Guardian* and other national newspapers and this can be very useful, not only because of the wide coverage but because of the cachet it bestows.

## Theatre Programmes

Ideally, few people could quarrel with the view that anyone who has bought a ticket for the performance has a right to know what is happening in it, and that therefore programmes should be free. Some theatres act in accordance with this and the delighted patrons have programmes provided for them without further charge. Bernard Shaw called charges for programmes and cloakroom fees "petty cadgings" and this is probably what we all feel.

The Royal Shakespeare Theatre, The National Theatre and Sadler's Wells have another attractive system. They issue a beautifully produced and very informative booklet of impressive size at a higher price than the normal theatre programme (and worth every penny) with a free cast list. This seems admirably to meet the needs of the two extreme opinions— that which says the barest essentials only are required, and that which argues that all possible background information about the play, the director, actors, designer, the author, previous productions, etc., is interesting and useful.

Most theatres have inherited an old tradition of relying on the income from advertisements to subsidize the printing of the programme and perhaps leave a little over. This was indeed necessary in the shoe-string days of the old-style repertory theatre, and the argument is still used that advertisements for local firms give good will. This kind of programme now, when the policy and practice of the more affluent and Arts-Council-supported theatres have radically changed, often fits very uncomfortably into the new scheme of things. There is a case for re-examining the style and content.

The phenomenon of "Playbill," an import from America, has established itself widely in the West End and is spreading into some regional theatres. It is perhaps too early to judge its real merit. The reduced cost of printing is a great attraction, but the regular theatregoer may well get very tired of thumbing through articles he has read in several other programmes to find the information that he seeks about the play he is about to see.

Whatever the style chosen, it is important here again that the theatre's chosen design and type style should if possible be carried through. The theatregoer is thus led by the posters in the town and his copy of the brochure to the display outside the theatre and the programme he receives inside. Hence the major importance of the initial choice of style and format, the recurring image of the theatre which will make its impression before even the ticket has been bought and which should be a harbinger in terms of the high standard of the theatre's aim and work.

### THE COMPILATION OF THE PROGRAMME

#### *Information about the Play*

The essential information to be conveyed about the play, is, of course, the cast list, the location of the action and division into acts and scenes. In this operation there must be the strictest accuracy. A safe rule is check, check and check again all the spellings, even if you think you know them, of the characters in the play and of the actors. Any mis-spelling ruins the whole thing, and can cause great annoyance to actors and their agents. Another trap is in the choice of a particular spelling among variants. Tchekov, for instance, appears in many guises. The final choice must be relentlessly checked so that it is standard in *all* publicity and press releases.

The division of the play into acts and scenes should be clearly indicated and the placing of the interval and its duration may be shown either in tabular form, e.g.

| | | | |
|---|---|---|---|
| Act I | Scene 1. | The Nursery. | Early morning |
| | Scene 2. | The Garden. | Evening |

INTERVAL OF TWELVE MINUTES

| | | | |
|---|---|---|---|
| Act II | Scene 1. | The Garden. | Next morning |
| | Scene 2. | The Same. | Two hours later |

Time: The present.

Or, if it is preferred to indicate the sequence of events straight through, by the note—

"There will be an interval of 12 minutes after Act 1."

There are many people who like to know how many intervals there are to decide about drinks or refreshments (especially if these can be ordered in advance) and to know how long they have to look at exhibitions or stroll around the theatre before warning bells begin to ring.

### Credits

This is the term for the acknowledgements to suppliers of costumes, wigs or special equipment or properties for the production, e.g.

Lighting equipment by Strand Electrical & Engineering Co. Ltd.

Swords by Bapty.            Stockings by Kayser Bondor.

These acknowledgements are sometimes required by the manufacturers and suppliers as a condition of the arrangement with the theatre. They are a recognized courtesy when special help has been given by local suppliers, and much appreciated as a particular form of advertising.

### Special Acknowledgements

1. It is usual in a programme to give clearly on a title page the name of the play, its author, the translator (if there is one), and the names of the director, the designer for scenery and/or costumes, the composer (particularly if the music has been specially composed), and it is now usual to include the lighting designer if his contribution to the production is important.

The title page usually carries also the title of the presenting management or the joint managements, with the appropriate phrase for the nature of their participation, e.g.—

X Productions in association with Y Productions

*or*

X Productions, by agreement with Y Productions

The phrase is usually laid down in the legal agreements between the managements who put on the play.

2. There may be an actor in the cast who has been temporarily released by another management or film company to whom he remains under long-term contract. Such an arrangement will require a note in the programme to the effect that—

> Mr. John Doe appears by kind permission of the . . . Film Organization Ltd. (*or* of the Governors of the . . . Theatre Company Ltd.)

This note should be in a prominent position as first of the acknowledgements, given below the information about the play itself, preceding the trade credits and isolated from them. The placing may be stipulated in the terms of the artist's contract.

3. There should be special acknowledgement of special financial help. For companies which receive subsidy from the Arts Council, a note to the effect that "X Players receive financial assistance from the Arts Council of Great Britain" is a requirement by the Council. Other sources of subsidy should be consulted about the need for a similar statement, since there are some who prefer not to have their help advertised; the phrasing must be agreed by both parties. This exact information is required because inaccuracy may infringe the conditions of the firms or foundations concerned or may give a wrong impression of the nature of the subsidy. It is a small courtesy to show in return for the value of the help received and the difficulty with which it may have been won. There are always people who are willing to seize on any apparently trivial error if they feel that subsidy should not have been given or is not being duly appreciated.

4. In notes about plays or authors, quotations may be used from critical works of scholarship, biographies or criticism of other productions. Care must be taken to check that permission can be obtained from the publisher on behalf of the author, or from the author himself, however brief the quotation from printed sources may be. Some payment may be needed, but in general it is true to say that

for the purpose of programmes with limited circulation sympathetic consideration is given to such requests. It is not always so sympathetic if the use of quotations is discovered *after* the event.

Quotations from critics' notices of the play are often used in programme notes and on posters, hand-outs, etc. This is generally allowed, provided that no changes or omissions are made which twist the impression intended by the writer. Acknowledgement of the source should be made.

Programmes of past productions are constantly needed for reference. It is a good idea to have the programmes for each year bound into a volume. These volumes are most useful and prevent loss of separate copies. They finally turn into valuable archives for the history of the company and its theatre.

### RELATIONS WITH THE PRESS

#### *The Press Release*

Theatre critics and newspaper editors are much maligned but any fault in unhappy relations between theatre and press often lies to a great degree with the theatre. The issuing of adequate advance information and the timing of these issues is of paramount importance, particularly for provincial theatres. While theatre critics are willing to travel out of London to see an increasingly wide range of productions, particularly of new plays, they have a very busy time and their main duty is to attend first nights in London. They therefore need to know as far ahead as possible about the dates of productions likely to interest them. The first important use for the press release is therefore to give advance warning, as soon as the dates are known, often before the issue of the theatre's printed folder of the season's schedule.

At this stage the names of key actors, perhaps of the designer or of other personnel may not be known. These can be supplied in a follow-up release, with as much information as possible about the play, the author, etc. Not all the information can always be used but it is better to give as much as possible rather than to be too selective. For local papers, paragraphs of more personal interest, likely to be of use as a news item or in a diary feature, are often very welcome to an editor who wants to give his readers interesting tit-bits and to help the theatre at the same time. This kind of information may catch the eye of those who do not necessarily read the more literary or specialized features.

The appearance of the press release is important. An avalanche of paper pours on to the desks of newspaper men all the time and if the theatre's press release is to compete effectively it helps if it is in some way distinctive. It could, for instance, be on coloured rather than white paper. It should have the name of the theatre boldly printed at the top and it is preferable to have one large sheet of paper (Size A4, perhaps) rather than two smaller sheets clipped together (and liable to come apart). It should never be printed on both sides, and please, never attempt to skimp on time or money by sending out shabbily duplicated sheets or bottom copies in shadowy and practically illegible typescript. Break up the information into short paragraphs, give headings and underlinings where these are helpful—in short, make the whole press release as attractive, as concise and as easy to read as possible for busy people.

## Press Tickets

Opinion varies about the manner of issuing press tickets, but in any event the invitation to attend should be sent to the Editor (*not* the critic personally, except by special arrangement) as early as possible, generally with the first press release.

Some theatres prefer to send a brief letter of invitation with the offer of two tickets to be collected from the Box Office on the night of the performance. This is particularly preferred by some provincial theatres because of the vagaries and delays, alas, of the postal service.

It is more usual to despatch the tickets for London performances direct and newspapers can usually be relied upon to return them if no critics can attend.

Critics have varying opinions about the need for examining the scripts of new plays or translations. If a request for the script is made, the theatre should make every effort to meet it, even though it is all too easy for scripts to be swallowed up early in the proceedings (some regrettably by actors who have been offered parts and refused!). Verbal information imparted to the local critic is a help to a busy man who may not have the time to see the play first.

The final and human follow-up to the issuing of press releases and all kinds of information to critics is a personal welcome by the theatre staff when the critic makes the pilgrimage into the provinces. The offer of a programme and possibly a drink in the interval will not be construed as a bribe but simply as a friendly appreciation of the effort made.

### RELATIONS WITH RADIO AND TELEVISION

The old complaint of the ousting of the theatre by these mass media which can be experienced in the home is now largely out of date. There are in fact several side-products which benefit the theatre in some ways. Viewers now become familiar with some great actors and great performances on their screens. Their experience of plays is enlarged, and, for example, the furore caused by *Cathy Come Home* was a proof of the impact a television play can have. There is no doubt of the forceful success of advertising on television and radio too has programmes which include comment, announcement and news items about musical, theatrical and artistic events in the regions.

It is possible, even probable, that theatres could profitably jettison a very great deal of their present mass of printed advertisements in exchange for a regular spot on radio and local television programmes. It is to be hoped that the authorities now being set up for local radio stations will bear local theatres, concert halls and art galleries very much in mind. These are the media of tomorrow. Radio and television could probably do more for promulgating interest in the arts than a trebling of the present expenditure in the theatre on the more old-fashioned material. This whole field of publicity for the theatre has still been only superficially explored.

### PUBLIC RELATIONS

The post of Public Relations Officer is of increasing importance, particularly in the regional theatres. At long last these theatres are able more seriously than ever before to examine their audience, both regular and potential, and to systematize ways of attracting various sections of the community to become regular patrons. Industry has set the pace and devised methods of consumer research and much of their achievement can usefully be reflected in theatre methods. This work of exploration and exploitation is the fascinatingly wide province of the PRO.

The field is wide and can be widened *ad infinitum* according to the dedication and initiative which are the main qualifications for this work. He must also possess the ability to get on good terms with the many kinds of people who are the key figures in the social, industrial and educational worlds around him and with those who, whether amateur or professional, are engeged in related spheres of cultural activity.

Some of the more important guide-lines are the following.

### 1. *Work with Young People*

As the present middle-aged generation of theatregoers grows older, a new and lively audience must be sought among the young. It is indubitable that teenagers usually tend to seek their pleasure elsewhere—on the telly, in their youth groups, in the coffee-house, or on their motor-bikes and in the dance hall. Paradoxically enough, it is to these young people that the dramatists of today, such as Joe Orton, Edward Bond, Cecil Taylor, and regional writers such as Peter Terson have something to say. It is also increasingly recognized in schools and training colleges that drama not only has a therapeutic value but that there is a great deal of creative energy which finds expression in group drama work—the build-up of a "living newspaper," improvisation of scenes and situations which can work out ideas and emotions relevant to their own lives, etc. The possibilities are endless and the results rewarding.

The introduction to the world of drama and the theatre can come in many ways through schools. Schools matinées of set plays bring examination work to life. Saturday morning classes of an informal nature, taken by the professional directors in many regional theatres, are very popular. Extra-mural visits to the theatre, requiring initiative by the child and supplementary to organized mass visits, can be made possible with the help of schools and educatoin authorities. Reduced prices for students whether at school, college, technical college or in further education, are a bait, but must never be regarded as a condescension. Visits by a lively company of young actors, as an off-shoot of the main company, can take the living theatre into schools, and thence, one hopes, may decoy the school children to normal theatre performances. Special Schools Days, when the production work in all its aspects is opened up for young audiences, show them how the wheels go round. The making of a production *in situ* can be a fascinating study and one that can be a help with future school productions. Young Supporters' groups can visit each other's theatres and meet their counterparts elsewhere.

The important proviso in all these activities is that they must be done without any suggestion of "talking down" to the young, who are quick to sense and resent any hint of "being done good to." The aim of the theatre as entertainment must never be lost sight of. Study in schools of plays in English and foreign languages can usefully be linked with the programmes of the local theatre, but should not be restricted to this aspect. It has become noticeable in the last few years that teachers are becoming more liberal and adventurous, and that school parties, perhaps of the Sixth form only (but this is a beginning), turn up to modern plays as well as to the set Shakespeare play. If these visits are followed up with intelligent and informal discussion, guided by a tactful and knowledgeable teacher, the horizon of taste and the potentiality of catholic enjoyment can be immeasurably widened.

The PRO will receive ready co-operation if he approaches in the right way all those concerned with education—the local education officers, teachers, youth-club leaders, drama advisers, etc. The ways in which the theatre and youth can meet together to their mutual advantage vary from place to place, but meeting points there are in plenty. Money too is forthcoming more readily now: from the Arts Council for special projects for young people and sometimes from the local authority. Theatre for youth in all its manifestations is a general concern.

## 2. *The Theatre and Industry*
It is perhaps the work of the Royal Shakespeare Company, both in Stratford and at the Aldwych Theatre, that has made

explicit the fruitful search for an audience in the big industrial concerns. Without going into detail, there are two main ways in which this relation can be explored. The first is in the establishment of regular bookings, via an official such as the Personnel or Entertainments Officer, subsidized by the firm, perhaps jointly with the theatre, but preferably regarded as a contribution by employers. The second is the invitation to spearhead groups, with specially devised programmes, such as the Royal Shakespeare's Theatre-go-round, to perform in the factory as well as in schools. This is intended to whet the appetite of the employees, and so break down the unfortunately prevailing image of the theatre as a sport of the leisured classes and the prerogative of a favoured minority.

There are still comparatively few theatres, even in their improved financial situation, which can afford the money for these activities and the extra staff and actors which are necessary. Here, as with the work for young people, there is a case for subsidy from industry, which looks nowadays to an increasingly close connection with the arts. It is an undisputed fact, explicitly demonstrated and proclaimed in the United States, that it is easier for an industry to attract bright young executives, for instance, if there are lively opportunities in drama, music and the arts in the area for themselves and their families, and the theatre can be the focal point.

### 3. *The Theatre's Contribution to the Community*

We tend to stress the decoying of audiences to the theatre, but what can the theatre give to the community, in addition to its programme, and to whom can it be given? Schools and factories provide a fairly captive audience, but there are other groups of adults drawn together by common interests which can be approached in rather the same way. The PRO must be ready to explore these and to form the manifold links which can keep a theatre in close touch with people of all ages and tastes. He will find that he will be called upon for numerous talks. The English are perhaps not quite so addicted to the lecture as, say, the Americans, but in every community many societies have a programme of guest speakers. He must be able to adjust his subject matter and his approach, as well as his jokes and anecdotes, to many different levels. The gamut of such societies varies very little in most towns and is likely to include the Rotarians, Soroptomists, Professional Women, Women's Institutes, day-release groups at Technical colleges, groups of graduate students, University societies, amateur dramatic and operatic societies.

For many of these the connection should go far beyond the spoken word. It may seem a great deal to ask of busy theatre people concerned with their own heavy and continuous pro-duction programme, but technical advice and help should always be readily and cheerfully given. The simplest and most often requested help is a visit to the theatre premises arranged through the PRO. Most people have a longing for "a peep behind the scenes," and those of us who take for granted the theatre as our lives, and for whom there is no mystique about backstage, must never under-estimate the pleasure that such a visit can give to those who have never been behind the curtain. These visits can be combined with a general talk on the policy and aims of the theatre, the logistics behind the choice of plays, etc. At the various strategic points the stage-manager, the electrician, the sound-operator, and, of course, the director, should be at hand to explain and answer questions on their particular departments.

Amateur societies present special problems. Members of the theatrical profession may often be heard to complain bitterly that amateurs are so busy putting on their own plays that they never bother to attend the professional productions. This may to a certain extent be true, but they are all nevertheless workers in the same field and the links between them cannot be ignored.

The PRO should make known to all the local amateur societies the facilities for which they may look to the professional theatre. Some theatres have a wardrobe hire service, which may be very useful to amateurs whose budget is tight and who may have no desire to build up a permanent wardrobe of their own. It may be possible sometimes to hire lighting equipment or sound-effect tapes and records not in current use. Advice above all is the commodity which is the cheapest but often the most valuable, and it should at all times be forthcoming. It does not always occur to amateur groups to ask for these things, and the PRO, in conjunction with the local Drama Adviser or Rural Community Council, should make known the theatre's willingness to help.

## 4. *Supporters' Clubs*

Groups directly concerned with the theatre and its activities flourished particularly strongly in the days of what might be termed "old style" repertory, the time when a small permanent company existed in many towns and became well known to and popular with the community within which they lived for long periods. The tendency is now to have a smaller nucleus only of permanent actors and actresses, recruiting others who come for particular plays. This is due partly to changes within the profession itself. Most actors of a certain calibre have lucrative extra employment from time to time in films and television, in which they can earn more money for comparatively few appearances than theatres can offer them over a season. They are therefore less willing to live for very long periods away from the focus of these activities in London. It is equally to the advantage of the theatres to take their opportunities of having actors who have made reputations in other media for guest appearances. Actors who have had their fill of the media with no live audiences yearn for an occasional return to the theatre, especially to play parts of their own choice which a regional theatre can offer them.

All this adds up to the fact that the rather cosy atmosphere of the supporters club has disappeared, the tea-parties, the fêtes, the get-togethers at which ordinary folk were able to meet and talk with the theatre personalities. Maybe television has destroyed some of the glamorous novelty now that figures of international repute are on the screen in our sitting rooms practically every night of the week, and magazines tell us far more than we want to know about their private lives and tastes.

Even so, theatres can still have the special groups of *aficionados* who want to work with and for the theatre. Through them, the season-ticket schemes for instance, which are the backbone of theatre audiences on the Continent, may be launched and built up with special privileges for members. Local folk may enjoy organizing special gala events in aid of new buildings, new equipment and redecoration, which are much needed but could not be squeezed out of the theatre's normal budget.

They thus experience the pleasure of special achievement with visible results.

The cardinal point about these enthusiasts is that they should not by their activities increase the work of the theatre, though they should be made to feel of real importance to it. The wise and tactful PRO should see to it that these clubs are run outside the theatre by some of the energetic and efficient people who have the time and the public spirit to take the burden of the work. The theatre premises might be able to include a special club-room, especially if a new building is planned with this in mind, as in the Yvonne Arnaud Theatre in Guildford. The theatre may from time to time be made available on Sundays, within the complicated regulations for genuine club activities. A fruitful relationship and one not too demanding for the theatre can be built up, and can unite profitably in a real preoccupation with the theatre's welfare many people who could not otherwise be brought together.

Supporters' clubs have their own organization, the Federation of Repertory Playgoers' Societies.

### 5. *Audience Surveys*

Stemming perhaps from the modern phenomenon of market research, the theatre manifests its interest in its audience by promulgating audience surveys. These have been undertaken by the big guns, such as the National Theatre, the Royal Shakespeare, the Royal Opera House and Sadler's Wells, and increasingly by theatres in the provinces. Let no one, however, be misled into thinking that cut-and-dried comprehensive results can be achieved by one single operation, however elaborate. Unlike the marketing of a product in industry, what the theatre has to offer is of changeable taffeta. Each play can be said to create its own audience to a certain extent. Those who flock to see a revival of a show cannot be counted on to return for a new play by an unknown author. The magic of a star name may carry an indifferent play on the tide of box-office success, while an interesting play with unknown actors, however good, may leave most seats woefully empty.

The questionnaire so trustfully distributed and so lovingly detailed by theatre managements is full of pitfalls. Not only is it an invitation to the joker, whose frivolous answers upset the statistics about forms filled up and returned, but it is full of hidden *snobisme* and social prejudice. Who is going to admit that he has attended his local theatre only once in the past year, and then for a revue? Who is willing to disclose his hatred of the kitchen sink when he has the lurking feeling that he is not "with it" if he does so?

I have stated clearly elsewhere, in a report for the Gulbenkian Foundation, that such surveys are best drawn up, distributed and interpreted by experts in this field—the sociologists, the statisticians, for instance, who should show us ourselves as others see us. We in the theatre are too deeply involved, and are unfamiliar with the pressures, the embarrassments and the omissions which lie behind the answers which we ask in good faith. A pilot scheme was in fact carried out by the Department of Sociology in the University of Sheffield, and much more could usefully be done. But it would be a long and expensive process, carried out not over a single season but over a number of years. It would change according to social changes and should keep pace with building and industrial developments in each area. Only then could the work be regarded as anything like a real evaluation of the chameleon taste which motivates any theatre's audience.

Dr. Peter Mann, Lecturer in Sociology, University of Sheffield, has published two very interesting articles which would be most helpful to any management contemplating organized research into an audience. They appeared in the *British Journal of Sociology:* in Volume XVII, No. 4, December 1966: "Surveying an audience: methodical problems"; and in Volume XVIII, No. 1, March 1967: "Surveying a theatre audience: findings." The second article concludes with a pointer for the future—

> Audience satisfaction is only crudely measured by box office returns; what is perhaps needed for theatre research is something akin to the BBC audience appreciation index which can indicate high degrees of satisfaction amongst an audience which may be comparatively small. As yet the theatre has brought no such social measurement.

*In Search of an Audience* by Bradley G. Morison and Kay Fliehr (Pitman Publishing Corporation, New York) gives a detailed description of how an audience was found for the Tyrone Guthrie Theatre in Minneapolis. Although the survey was conducted by the authors with application of American techniques that are not in all respects appropriate to the British market, the book is one that is well worth study.

This section has dealt with public relations hitched to the wagon of the PRO. In a sense every one in the theatre shares his job and contributes to it. The physical impression of the building, its appeal to the eye and its comfort and cleanliness are important factors. For the public, encounters with the staff, whoever they may be and whatever their jobs, must be pleasant. Above all, the Director of Productions and the Administrator, who know only too well that the theatre cannot please all the people all the time, must plan the programme to cater for varied tastes.

If the tenuous hold on the public is to be maintained, only the best is good enough, in all departments. Local councillors arguing against subsidy for the arts often say that the theatre, the art gallery, and the concert hall are not necessities. All who work in the theatre must be of the sincere belief that art is a necessity and must so work that for an increasing number of the public it becomes an addiction, something which they cannot do without if they want a window on worlds outside their ordinary lives.

# 22

# THE BOX OFFICE

IT seems logical to examine the staff and system in a box office as part of the public relations picture, since it is at this all-important focal point front-of-house that the public gain the first impression of the theatre. No less than the Administrator and his immediate assistants, the box-office staff need personal as well as professional qualifications. The Gorgon behind the *guichet*, unwillingly interrupting a conversation with her colleagues to parley with the interrupter who dares to want a ticket, is a vanishing figure and rightly so. The personal contact needed in the modern theatre calls for people more knowledgeable about plays and policy and more ready to volunteer information. The prospective customer is no longer necessarily a regular theatregoer but needs to be tempted and convinced. Young people, for all the brashness of which they are accused, can in fact be easily intimidated. There is the burden of choice, whether or not the play is suitable, where the seats on offer are situated in relation to the stage, etc. None of this must be made to appear a mystique for the initiated only or calculated to make a young man lose face with his girl-friend. Luckily, modern theatre planning is inclined to open up the box office to make it more like, say, the counter of a travel bureau and less like a cell which offers communication with the public only through a forbidding grille. Perhaps a radical change in the whole method of issuing tickets may soon be adopted in theatres, on the lines of the computerized airline method. In the meanwhile, and probably for a long time yet, most of us will have to continue with our present box offices and staff.

### THE SYSTEM

Slow and clumsy though it may appear by modern standards, the basic system of using a plan for each performance, with books of tickets with two counterfoils and the main section giving date, seat and row numbers and possibly time of performances, has a great deal to be said for it. Each theatre has its own variations of the system but the essential principles are straightforward, easily checkable, need comparatively little bookkeeping and ancillary material, and interlock sufficiently to make errors traceable without difficulty. For convenience this system is set out, with specimen return sheets, etc., in Appendix 1.

The box-office staff should have the following qualities and qualifications—

1. Ability to deal accurately and efficiently with the bookkeeping required. An essential point in the system is the accurate marking of the plan correlated with the automatic checking after each booking, whether personally by post or by telephone, of the date, the number and price of the tickets required. Elementary as this may sound, it is necessary for the pinning down of the surprising number of people who airily say "Tickets for next Wednesday" with the firm conviction that next Wednesday is the 8th of the month instead of the 9th, or "today week" under the impression that "today" is Monday instead of Tuesday.

2. Discretion in deciding when it is necessary to refuse favours in the matter of exchanging tickets, and the occasion for indulgence to regular patrons.

3. A good memory for faces. Nothing pleases regular patrons more than to be greeted and offered seats in their favourite position in the theatre.

4. Absolute trustworthiness. Trust goes without saying, since most systems, however efficient, are susceptible to human error whether accidental or designed.

5. A quality all too often ignored by the management—the genuine interest in the play or the company which enables the box-office staff to give an intelligent account of the production or information, within reason, about the actors. It is essential that the box-office staff should be as fully briefed as possible. They, more than anyone else in the theatre, are asked direct questions about the play, whether it is "suitable," etc. A hesitant patron should never be

"conned" into buying a ticket, but many are grateful for the factual information which may help them to make up their minds.

6. Patience and interest in people. The box office can be a valuable barometer of opinion since comments are made casually and freely which might never be formally expressed to the management.

A note for the Administrator and House Manager: if a patron genuinely finds a play offensive and comes out before the end of the play angrily demanding his money back, it is rarely advisable to embark on an argument about aesthetics. The reasons for choosing the play as worthy of production can be firmly stated but the money should then be given back without more ado.

## THE PLANNING OF THE BOX-OFFICE PREMISES

Considering the importance of the box office in the hierarchy of theatre staff, the physical conditions in which they work are rarely easy. All too often, even in new buildings, it is assumed that they need only a cubby-hole to work in. In fact, to store adequately their plans, stationery, brochures of the theatre's programmes—sometimes even programmes—they need a lot of storage space. They need on their actual counters a large area for the theatre plans, especially when booking for several plays at a time is in progress. The ease of access to the books of tickets should be made as efficient as possible to reduce the risk of giving tickets from the wrong one, which is all too easy. There should be space for one member of staff to deal with postal booking while another deals personally with customers at the window. Telephones should be easy to reach, so that the plans may be consulted and details written for a telephone booking. Tickets, plans and telephone should all be correctly placed so that one person may deal with all three without moving. Most of the staff's day is spent sitting in one chair at the window, so the chair and the height of the counter must be comfortably planned.

There are some arguments in favour of an open box-office, but strong counter-arguments in favour of making it difficult, if not impossible, for those booking tickets to read the names on the plan or to argue about apparently vacant spaces which may be reserved for a special reason. A more homely argument is for the protection of the staff from the coughs and sneezes and tobacco smoke with which they are constantly assailed. The box office of the Royal Opera House, Covent Garden, is very much on new and interesting lines and there is an article on it by the present writer in the ABTT Newsletter (Summer, 1968).

There is a scheme afoot, to be promoted in Great Britain by an American firm, to introduce computerized electronic box offices which would render obsolete our present methods if it could be installed widely or at least in the larger cities. Ticket Reservation Systems, Inc., of New York have already started in that city, with proposals to link up Los Angeles and Chicago in a later phase. It could eventually be possible to link up cities in Britain so that theatre tickets could be bought not only in each country but trans-Atlantically too.

With this system the terminals in selected agencies, hotels, stores, etc., are all linked with a central computer. This in its turn is linked with terminals in the box-offices of the theatres concerned. Information programmed into the central computer can be selected by any remote terminal. When a prospective ticket-buyer inquires for tickets, indicating price and location in the theatre, information about the seats available is fed back, and when he has made his decision, the actual ticket is printed out on the spot. This information is then recorded by the central computer, the tickets purchased are withdrawn and there is no possibility of selling the tickets again.

This makes the process of buying theatre tickets more like that of buying an airline ticket, efficient and impersonal. Presumably it would also cope with exchanges or the other vicissitudes of box-office operation, and could eliminate much of the book-keeping. It would also eliminate some of the personal relationships which grow up between theatres and their clients, the loss of which relationship many would regret. Against this the company claims that sales increase to those who would not make a special trip to the theatre to buy tickets but will include them on a general shopping list. It is claimed also that the mechanical process provides the public with the assurance that the best seats actually available are being offered, without any suspicion, which commonly exists, that box-office staff withhold some tickets for nefarious purposes of their own.

A computerized system for mailing lists also has recently been examined by the T.M.A. Both this and the box-office scheme are likely to be costly, but some advance of science into this field of theatre is probably inevitable, with all its advantages and disadvantages. The qualities and qualifications of the computer-operator will then have to be included in any future review of theatre administration!

# 23

## *THE ACCOUNTANT*

THE control of finance used to be part of the province of the administrator in the repertory theatre. With the greatly increased sums of money involved, derived from higher box office prices, subsidy from the Arts Council and other sources, together with the multifarious projects such as touring, educational activities, operation of transport subsidies, etc., it is now, in most theatres of any stature, necessary to have a full-time Accountant.

His job mirrors the two-fold financial picture—the day-to-day running according to a budget of income and expenditure and the forward planning of continuation and development of policy. He works with the Artistic Director and Administrator, translating into monetary terms the dreams of one and the inescapable responsibilities of the other. With these two also he is responsible to the theatre's Board of Directors, to whom he should at any time be able to give an accurate and up-to-the-minute account of the theatre's trading position and its relation to the estimates.

Taking the two categories, his duties include the following—

### DAY-TO-DAY RUNNING

It must be assumed, since the process has to start somewhere, that he is working on an agreed estimate of income and expenditure, and that the company is in full operation in a theatre producing plays.

### 1. *Payment of Salaries and Wages*
He will make all payments to employees according to their contracts of employment, having access to such a contract for everyone in full-time employment with the company. This involves—

Computing and deduction of income tax if the employee is on the PAYE scheme, and the proper filling up of tax forms for employees leaving.

The operation of Selective Employment Tax and claiming for its repayment to the company if this is applicable.

Deduction of National Insurance and Graduated Pensions from the gross salary.

The purchase of insurance stamps for all cards and their proper attachment and cancellation on the cards.

The preparation of statements of money earned and payments made as required by Government Departments for all employees at the end of the financial year.

The computing of overtime payments according to contract terms and union rules.

The payment of holiday money according to the length of employment and other terms laid down by Equity.

The payment of all special fees, royalties, copyright licence fees, legal fees, indeed any and all financial liabilities to individuals, firms, agents, and other managements, etc.

Deductions or other adjustments to payments required by illness or accident. He must be careful that accidents are properly recorded in a special Accident Book kept by the Administrator in which details are entered and signed by the Administrator and the victim. This is necessary in case of dispute in industrial accident claims when the victim is working in the theatre at the time.

The operation of the pension scheme which most theatres now have in one form or another. Details of these schemes can be obtained from the Council or Repertory Theatres or from an insurance company which the management may prefer to consult.

### 2. *Production Payments*

He is responsible for receiving, checking, filing and recording all order forms, advice notes, invoices and statements. This can be made effective by a system of order forms in triplicate (or even more copies) of which he will receive a copy relating to purchases in all departments. If a statement of the financial position at a special date is required, reference to this system will enable him to see what liability is incurred for goods not yet received. There are some accounting systems which make allowance for this.

All the appropriate journals, ledgers, cash-books, etc., for the chosen system must be kept completely and methodically up-to-date.

### 3. *Standing Charges*

In the preparation of any statement of expenditure, it is possible to compute a standard figure, a weekly or monthly average over the year, for some of the overhead costs, e.g. insurance, legal charges, heating, lighting, etc., which are constant but not attributable to any production and which appertain even during a period when the theatre is closed. This figure should appear in any production statement in addition to the particular and variable costs.

### 4. *Production Accounts*

Soon after the end of each production it should be possible to produce a statement of the actual income and expenditure on that particular production, plus the standing charges for the period of its run. The account should include on the expenditure side the pre-production costs, i.e. every expense incurred during the rehearsal period, and the running costs, preferably under these separate headings.

On the income side, the box-office receipts naturally appear, together with a related proportion of the Arts Council grant and other subsidy.

It is useful to work out for each production the percentage of attendance and the percentage of the total financial capacity. The two are not necessarily the same, since some productions not playing to capacity may attract a majority in number to either the cheaper or the more expensive seats. Some useful information may be deduced from these percentages, though there are other factors to be taken into account also.

Theatres presenting plays in repertoire present special problems in the unravelling of expenditure on separate productions. It is rarely, for instance, that the dovetailing of the entire company is complete from play to play. Moreover, costs for casual labour and overtime in shifting and re-setting from play to play have to be apportioned, and there may be overlapping expenditure in several departments. If there can be flexibility in the programme, allowing for the extension of the numbers of performances of a success and the reduction of the number of performances of a less successful one, the long-term financial result will be good but the immediate accountancy more difficult.

In deciding the methods of operating the accounting system for a repertoire programme, the guiding principle is to be consistent. Whichever way is chosen as the best for apportioning the costs and income, pursue it in detail and completely. This will satisfy the auditors and should present a true picture of results overall.

### 5. *Interim Statements*

While the production accounts are of great importance in the operation of the artistic policy, statements of the company's financial situation should be issued at regular intervals, say monthly. It is useful if this statement can be under the standard headings used in all calculations: the estimates, production accounts, the cheque payments book, petty cash, etc. It is then possible to put the estimated figure beside the columns to act as a check or a brake. Such statements are a great help to the Arts Council if subsidy is involved.

### FORWARD PLANNING

### 1. *Estimates*

Expansion goes on apace in most theatres and the raising of standards, which should be their constant aim, means the need for more money. All bodies which give subsidy need to plan their own requirements. The Arts Council and the Treasury, for instance, have somehow to try to align what is asked for and what can be given from Government funds. Local authorities have to review all their areas for public spending, the arts among them. While new ideas are favourably considered according to their merits, as much notice as possible is needed in the form of estimates. These should be realistic. There is no point in trying to duck an impressive figure lest it should be turned down. This either results in the final abandonment of a project or its partial failure, which puts paid to any thought of repeating it in a more efficient form. Nor is it generally advisable to double the number you first thought of, believing you are then sure of getting half. The estimates go forward for expert scrutiny and reasonable allowance is usually made for contingencies if the basic calculations are seen to be sound.

The estimates should also be based on a realistic box-office assessment, and the ratio between box-office expectation and hoped-for subsidy must be reasonable. Every effort must be made in the way of self-help, by seeking to increase the audience without unduly increasing staff or overheads. A rise in ticket prices must be carefully considered—it may not be a wise move but at the same time the burden must not be left entirely to the outside bodies.

Constant rises in the cost of materials, supplies and services are bound to occur, but remember that something which has an effect on the general public, such as a rise in postage or telephone costs, cannot be fully anticipated in an individual budget and cannot be allowed too extensively as a legitimate contingency. It will be taken into account, one hopes, at the source in Government planning including provision for the arts.

### 2. *Capital Expenditure*

Part of the company's expansion involves at one time or another the acquisition of new equipment, front-of-house or backstage, or of additional premises and their furnishings and fittings. These are legitimate expenses according to the conditions of a non-profit-distributing company, and, after the writing-off of agreed depreciation, can be shown as part of the company's assets. The expenditure of large sums must of course be done with the full knowledge and consent of the Theatre Board, and the information made known also to any other interested parties.

### 3. *The Balance-sheet*

As the forward estimates are the prediction of the company's future, so the balance-sheet mirrors the truth and accuracy of the forecast. A balance-sheet must be prepared annually by the accountant working with the auditors appointed to the company. He must make available to them all the books of the company with supporting vouchers and related material. The balance-sheet must be passed by the Directors of the Company and the Theatre Board, if they are not one and the same body, and presented to a General Meeting of the members of the Company formally called according to the Memorandum and Articles of Association. The balance-sheet must be open to inspection as a true record of the company's trading situation.

# 24

## THEATRE FINANCE

THE image of theatre people as helplessly and hopelessly un-
practical about money could not be less realistic. The progress
of a theatre is subject to all kinds of hazards. As sensitively as
the Stock Exchange, it reflects any hint of national recession.
Wars and rumours of wars have an incalculable effect on
theatregoing. The sudden heat-wave which rejoices the hearts
of families bound for the sea-side or enjoying their gardens
will leave the theatre manager wringing his hands over a plum-
meting attendance. The hopefully planned production, packed
with star performers and expensively mounted, may, for in-
scrutable reasons, simply not "catch on." All or any of these
factors may send even the best-planned budgeting agley.
Nevertheless, the realistic and accurate budget, whether for
one production by an amateur group or for a whole season by
a repertory company, is the heart of the matter.

The theatre manager must therefore be something of an
accountant (as well as something of a clairvoyant, if possible!).
He is finally responsible to his Board of Management for the
current and future financial situation of his theatre, and to all
his employees individually for a fair deal and adequate working
conditions within the building, so far as his money will stretch.
He must also be a diplomat and often a tough negotiator to
weigh the claims of an artistic director, insisting that without
some highly expensive equipment the whole production will
be a disaster, against the future planning of other plays for
which this sum of money is urgently necessary for the bare
essentials of presentation.

The control of finance really brings into play all the skills
and qualities which a manager should possess. Artistic understanding can help him in discussions with those responsible for
the choice of plays and the manner and style of production.
Understanding of technical matters can enable him to assess the

needs for new or special equipment. Concern for his audience and for the "image" of the theatre enables him to balance the stage expenditure against the front of house needs for re-decoration or a new carpet. The essential qualities in these dilemmas are probably honesty in his dealings with all the personnel, so that they are aware of the motives behind his decisions and frankness in explaining the problems. There is very rarely, to my mind, any need to conceal from the staff the financial factors which govern the whole conduct of the theatre. This said, how to get down to the hard facts?

### BUDGETING A PRODUCTION

It must be borne in mind that the income and expenditure for each individual production must be carefully and conservatively estimated. This applies no matter whether it is one production in a season of many plays or whether, as is often the case with an amateur society, it is a single annual event. The manager planning a varied season must obviously be guided by the financial results of what has gone before and the needs and probable revenue of what has to follow. Risks have to be taken but as few as possible: they should be carefully calculated risks. It will be known that the public appeal of certain productions will be less than others and the expenditure should be estimated accordingly. There may be very good reasons why a loss on a particular production is a justifiable risk but the risk should be taken with a clear recognition of its probable effect on the financial position as a whole and not in an excess of reckless enthusiasm. The principles are, briefly—

### 1. RECEIPTS

For a theatre or production company working all the year round with a varied programme the usual practice is to work in an average figure for the receipts, made up of the proportion of income which can reasonably be expected, e.g—

    (i) Box-office receipts, say 60 per cent of average.
    (ii) Proportion of Arts Council grant or other subsidy.
    (iii) Proportion of profit on front-of-house rights (programmes, bars, etc.).

These proportionate figures should be on the conservative side if anything, so that the annual total takes account of the overwhelming success with full houses and the unexpected failures, which naturally reduce the front-of-house income dependent on attendance.

## 2. PROVISIONAL BUDGET

Provisional budget, i.e. the physical preparation of the production, rehearsal costs, etc., as distinct from costs incurred during the running period.

Decide firmly on the maximum figure to be expended on production costs. Make it conservative and add a percentage of the total extracted from the detailed categories, say 5 or 10 per cent for "contingencies." This is not a device for covering inaccurate budgeting but an allowance for the effects of heat-wave in the summer or fog in the winter, illness, or an unexpected rise in the cost of some commodity. It is *not* an open invitation to the designer to buy ring velvet instead of furnishing material or to the director to hire a string quartet!

## 3. PRESENTING THE BUDGET

Having decided on the figures, call together the heads of departments, i.e. set designer, costumes designer, wardrobe mistress and stage-manager, and impart to them the figures on which they must work. Their views must be aired fully. If the manager is convinced by them that the figures offered are unrealistic and insufficient, he should give way to expert opinion if he is satisfied that it is reasonable. It is no use demanding the impossible. If a very tight budget is inescapable he may send the staff away to think again about cheaper alternatives, or ways of robbing Peter to pay Paul, e.g. reducing the costume budget in favour of the set or taking out the hire of special effects in stage-management to provide more elaborate costumes. Only when all the avenues are fully explored and to everyone's satisfaction (if this is ever possible!) can the provisional figures be finalized. The Administrator's dictum must be final since he alone can at any stage take the long view about finance. This is, of course, the point where it is absolutely essential for the Administrator and the Artistic Director to understand each other's views and responsibilities and to have a well-planned programme in mind without too much rocking of either's boat.

4. CONTROLLING THE BUDGET

When all are satisfied that the amounts allotted for expenditure in all the production departments are fair (they are never thought to be generous) some form of check must be instituted to ensure that the totals finally will be within the parish. The rate of progress should be ascertainable at any given moment through the following—

(i) *Running Total of Expenditure already incurred*

The heads of departments are often too closely involved in the production preparations under pressure of time to keep accurate account of the payments made and payments incurred through forward ordering. It is therefore the task of the accountant, if the theatre is so fortunate as to have one who looks after day-to-day running, or of the Administrator if the task falls to him, to keep as accurately as possible a running total which can be compared with the budget. The easiest way is to institute a system of collecting weekly from all departments, at a set time, the multifarious invoices, receipts for cash payments and forward order forms, and correlating them. Early warning can be given if expenditure is catching up too fast with the budgeted figure and decisions can be made about last-minute requests (inevitable, alas!) for extra expenditure.

(ii) *Order Forms*

While it is comparatively easy to assess the situation from bills receipted and cash payments with vouchers in corroboration, there may be some difficulty in taking into due account material and supplies on order, for which invoices have not yet been received.

Order books, in triplicate, are the answer. They should be used for all orders to firms with which the theatre has accounts, should state clearly the details of what is required, and should bear the signature of the person responsible for the order. It is essential, if this system is to operate effectively, that both suppliers and the staff who order should understand that orders will not be accepted without an accredited signature and that

the number of signatures is limited to a few responsible persons,
e.g. the theatre manager, the production manager and the
designer. Chaos reigns if all and sundry send in orders, con-
fusing the firms and making nonsense of budget control.

The forms in triplicate are necessary, so that one reaches
the supplier, one reaches the general office for the information
and signature of the manager or accountant, and the third
remains in the book as a record. Ideally, if the system were
to be completely water-tight, every order should be countersigned by the manager or the accountant. In practice, with the
speed at which things happen and the diversity of theatre-work,
this would be asking the impossible, but it should be enforced
as far as the limits will go.

## ACCOUNTING SYSTEMS

Each theatre management has theories about the ideal accounting system and no hard and fast rule can be laid down. The
essential requirements are that any system should keep an exact
record of all details and that it should be possible to extract
statistics at will and at once. For anyone who has the good
fortune to be starting a company or a theatre from scratch,
it is well worth investigating a really first-class system to be
instituted as part of the capital cost, considerable as this may be.

For those of us who are not so well-placed, or have not the
initial cost to hand, the following are the minimum requirements for a theatre accounting system—

1. *A Cheque Payments Book* to record the cheque number and
total of each cheque drawn, with as many columns as possible
for the analysis of the nature of the expenditure, indicating
the production or productions to which the amounts refer.
This book is used for checking the bank statement.
2. *A Journal* for the entry of invoices received.
3. *Income and Expenditure summary.*
4. *Files* for invoices, statements, receipts.
5. *Petty Cash Book*, analysed as far as possible in line with
the headings in the main cheque payments book.
6. The *Order Books* referred to above, annotated as clearly

as possible with reference to productions and allocated to heads of departments.

7. *Books for the running totals* for each production.

8. *Salaries and Wages Book.*

Two main principles to be borne in mind are as follows.

### (i) *Ease of Reference*

Whatever system is adopted, it must be reasonably easy to handle. It will be useful only in so far as it can provide accurately and quickly information in any form required.

It should also be able to supply answers to any other financial queries. For instance, the Publicity Manager may wish to change his printer and would need to know the exact costs of the standing arrangement over a certain period. The Stage Director may find a potential new supplier and would like to know the amounts spent to date with the current suppliers of a particular commodity. The Administrator might consider changing to contract cleaning if he cannot find enough efficient Mrs. Mopps and would like to add his cleaning staff's wages to the total of cleaning and maintenance supplies to weigh the relative costs. The possibilities are endless, and there is no time in the day-to-day business of a theatre to spend hours hunting in inadequate or inaccurate records. There are the statutory returns of tax deductions, and individual statements of cash earned, PAYE, SET, etc., which all have to be done willy-nilly and which take very little time with a good system and an unconscionably long time with a vague one.

### (ii) *Detailed Analysis*

This is really a corollary of the easy-reference requirement. A 36-column account book may look formidable, but remarkably enough there are seldom enough columns in the largest account book to cater for all the analysis which should be made. Never rely on the column headed "Miscellaneous" to solve your problems! It will only create more for you. This should, in fact, be the column with the fewest entries and the smallest total, if you wish to avoid the puzzle of a large discrepancy between the production accounts individually or the grand total of the season's expenditure, or that of the financial year. "Miscellaneous" is also a term which is a red rag to an auditor.

**Proposed Budget: 1969–70**

|  | Actual 1968–9 | Budgeted | Proposed 1969–70 |
|---|---|---|---|
| **INCOME** | | | |
| 1. Series tickets | | | |
| 2. Single sales | | | |
| 3. Programme advertising | | | |
| 4. Concessions | | | |
| 5. Other productions | | | |
| 6. Miscellaneous | | | |
| 7. TOTAL INCOME | | | |
| **EXPENSES** | | | |
| 8. Salaries and Social Security | | | |
| *Programme* | | | |
| 9. Scenery | | | |
| 10. Lighting | | | |
| 11. Properties | | | |
| 12. Costumes | | | |
| 13. Musicians, Music | | | |
| 14. Scripts | | | |
| 15. Royalties | | | |
| 16. Advertising, Publicity | | | |
| 17. Box Office | | | |
| 18. Programmes | | | |
| 19. Tickets | | | |
| 20. Theatre rental | | | |
| 21. Other | | | |
| 22. SUB-TOTAL | | | |
| *Building* | | | |
| 23. Utilities | | | |
| 24. Maintenance | | | |
| 25. Insurance | | | |
| 26. Repairs | | | |
| 27. SUB-TOTAL | | | |
| *Administration* | | | |
| 28. Office supplies | | | |
| 29. Postage | | | |
| 30. Telephone and telegraph | | | |
| 31. Dues and subscriptions | | | |
| 32. Audit and legal | | | |
| 33. Directors' expenses | | | |
| 34. Others | | | |
| 35. SUB-TOTAL | | | |
| TOTAL EXPENSES | | | |
| NET INCOME | | | |
| CASH BALANCE: START OF YEAR | | | |
| CASH BALANCE: END OF YEAR | | | |

## Categories

### Income Sources
Series memberships
Children's theatre
Student performances
Concessions
Sales and rental
Special performances
Group sales
Theatre school
Programme ads.
Touring productions
Summer season

### Administrative Schedule
Box office
Promotion and publicity
Office supplies
Telephone and telegraph
Postage
Answering service
Local expenses for staff
Dues and subscriptions
Membership campaign
  (Season)
Group sales campaign
Audit and legal
Equipment replacement
Theatre equipment
Lighting and sound equip-
  ment
Office equipment

### Building
Utilities
Maintenance
Insurance
Repairs
Storage

### Production costs
Scripts
Royalties
Staging: scenery, lights, props.
Costumes
Tickets
Programme
Musicians, music
Outside presentations
Transportation
Summer Season
Theatre rental

### Staff salaries and Social Security
Managing director
Visiting production directors
Business manager
Public relations director
Art director
Stage manager
Technical director
Wardrobe mistress
Box-office manager
Secretaries
Assistants
Actors and actresses
Seamstress
Apprentices
Social Security

### Education
Children's theatre
Theatre school

## CATEGORIES OF EXPENDITURE

There are various requirements for theatres which may operate in slightly different ways, e.g. weekly, fortnightly or in repertoire (i.e. playing two or three productions each for, say, a few days at a time over a period, as is done by the big national companies, and also by some of the larger provincial companies, e.g. Nottingham and Oxford). The larger the company and the longer its seasonal period, of course, the more elaborate the accounting system needs to be.

In general, for small companies, and for individual productions, amateur and professional, the following suggestions may provide a working basis—

*Category* 1. *Pre-production costs.* All costs incurred during the rehearsal period.

*Category* 2. *Production costs.* All costs incurred while the production is running in the theatre, either the base theatre or on tour.

*Category* 3. *Standing charges.*

*Category* 4. *General and Premises costs.*

1. *Pre-production and Production Costs* (Categories 1 and 2)—

Set
Properties and dressings for set (purchases and hires)
Costumes (purchases and hires)
Extra lighting or effects
Music-copying or hired scores recording, etc.
Scripts (purchase or copying)
Transport
Travel
Extra rents—rehearsal room, recording studios, etc.
Stage management petty cash
Royalties
Special publicity and printing
Casual labour: get-in and fit-up costs

## 2. *Standing Charges* (Category 3)

### (Exclusive of premises and administration)

These are the costs which have to be met regularly regardless of productions or the income and expenditure specifically related to productions. It is usual to work out a proportionate figure for a week or for a specified period and to add this figure regularly to the costs of each production. The items to be allocated include for instance—

> Insurance—for the physical production and to the person
> Theatre rent
> Rates
> Legal fees
> Audit fees
> Licence
> Subscriptions to professional bodies

## 3. *General Costs* (Category 4)

In a theatre operating regularly, the total of these costs can also be averaged out per week or over a special period and must be added, like those of Category 3, to the costs of productions to show the theatre's full operating costs. The items to be allocated under this heading include—

| *Permanent staff salaries* | Administrator |
|---|---|
| | Assistant |
| | Secretary |
| | Box office |
| | Cleaners etc. |

| *Premises costs* | Heat |
|---|---|
| | Light |
| | Water |
| | Power |
| | Insurance |

*Repairs and maintenance—*

*Administrative costs*      Printing—tickets, programmes, etc.
Publicity—regular advertisements,
     newspaper advertisements, etc.
Stationery
Postage
Telephone
Management travel
Official entertainment
Office petty cash
Office furniture and equipment

*Equipment,* capital expenditure, replacements, repairs.
*Materials and supplies,* stage and front-of-house (recurrent)

### BUDGET SUMMARY

A suggested budget summary, with figures for the previous year
as a comparison, together with check lists for income and
expenditure, are given on the previous pages.

### THEATRE INCOME

The main sources of theatre income in the subsidized theatres
vary, of course, with the locale. Some local authorities
subsidize their theatre in more than one way, in others local
industry takes a practical interest.
     The main sources are—

*External subsidy:*      Local Authority: direct grant or guarantee
         against loss via education authority
Local industry
Arts Council of Great Britain

*Internal revenue:*  Box office
Catering
Sale of programmes
Sale of ancillary material—postcards, books, magazines, scores, etc.
Hire of wardrobe, properties, lighting and sound services which are owned by the theatre

INTERNAL REVENUE

*Box Office*
The range of prices in the regional theatres is comparatively low, as the following examples show (as at 31 March, 1968)—

| | |
|---|---|
| Bristol Old Vic | 3s.; 4s.; 7s.; 9s.; 10s.; 12s. (season ticket scheme) |
| Bristol Little | 3s. 6d.; 5s.; 7s.; 8s. 6d. |
| Belgrade Coventry | 4s. 6d.; 6s. 6d.; 9s. 6d.; 8s. |
| Castle, Farnham | 4s.; 7s. 6d. |
| Phoenix, Leicester | 6s.; 7s. 6d.; 8s. 6d. |
| University Theatre Manchester | Professional: 6s. 6d.; 9s. 6d.; 12s. 6d. University: from 4s. 6d.; 9s. 6d. |
| Nottingham Playhouse | 5s.; 7s. 6d.; 8s. 6d.; 10s. |
| Oxford | Professional: 5s.; 8s.; 11s. University: 4s.; 5s. 6d.; 7s.; 9s. |
| Victoria, Stoke-on-Trent | 4s.; 7s.; Children 3s. 6d. |

Some of these have increased prices, average 1s. extra, on Saturday nights.

Even these prices show a remarkable increase over the last few years, though not necessarily comparable with the rise in the cost of living. Not all of us would go all the way with the sentiment once expressed by Peter Brook that, as everything else becomes more expensive, so theatre prices should become less so, but we all see the idea behind this exaggeration. Theatre remains a minority interest and if it were to charge prices which would meet all the costs of running a theatre and mounting productions while playing on an average to less than capacity, it would price itself out of the market. The question is still asked in Britain, though not in continental countries, where theatre is taken for granted as an essential part of a way of life: "Why do the arts need subsidy? Why can they not be self-supporting?"

Apart from the built-in aesthetic problem in the question, the examination of the balance sheets of any of the subsidized theatres, national or regional, would show the discrepancy that exists between the costs which must be met to provide theatre of a significant standard and the box-office receipts which can be expected over a reasonably successful season.

The question of the ratio of subsidy to box-office income is fascinating, but too complex in statistical terms to be dilated upon here. Some of the principles to be borne in mind for his box office by the Administrator may be summarized as follows—

1. *Price fixing.* Decide on an equitable distribution of prices fairly related to the degree of good view of the stage.

Do not, except for special ocasions such as opera, alter the distribution or raise the prices. The public soon become used to paying a set price for a particular seat and become suspicious if there is frequent variation.

2. *Reduced prices for first nights.* The lure of cheap prices can appeal and build up an audience for days of the week when attendance may not be so good, e.g. the first part of the week, or first nights of new plays, since many unadventurous spirits wait for the critic's reports. It is often a good thing, therefore, especially for the actors who like to be aware of their audience, to have a cheap price overall, on say, Mondays and first nights. The audience, large or small, is then built up from the front of the house instead of being concentrated in the cheaper seats at the back of the auditorium.

*Note:* Difficulties may occur in plays presented in repertoire, when the first night of a play may occur mid-week. All one can do is to establish the principle of cheap first nights, if that is the theatre policy, whenever these may occur.

The audience has in any case to adjust itself to taking note of the dates of the programme in repertoire, and this will soon be part of its expectations.

Secondly, if the principle of cheap first nights is established, be generous, and do not withdraw from this bargain with the audience if you suddenly acquire a famous star who will fill the house in any case. It may seem gratutitous generosity, but you must remember the more frequent occasions when you need the audience for less popular plays. The generous gesture can only increase good will and theatres need all that they can get of this commodity.

3. *Season tickets.* We should all like to be in the happy situation of theatres abroad, in Germany, say, where the bulk of the tickets are sold to regular subscribers before the season even begins, notably in the opera-houses. Most theatres in Britain have at one time or another embarked on a season-ticket or regular booking scheme, with variable success. Neither current social habits nor the present *modus operandi* of the theatre seem conducive to this regular habit. It worked to a certain extent in the past in "old-style" repertory—the regular presentation of well-known plays, weekly or fortnightly by a regular company. Socially, the theatre had not in those days quite so many effective competitors and there was not such a wide choice of entertainment. We have now broken up the small company which stayed together for a year or more by bringing in more guest stars, varying our programmes by choosing actors for plays rather than plays to fit an existing company of actors. Our freedom of choice is greater too, and our range of plays is wider. We are encouraged by the standard-setting of our actors, our dramatists and those who subsidize us to be more adventurous in our choice of plays, not all of which are immediately acceptable to our audiences. Many people would refuse to be bound by the possession of a season ticket to see what they might term a kitchen-sink drama; others abhor particular classical dramatists, even Shakespeare.

Although it militates against regular theatre-going, the right to choose and to reject is finally a good thing. It affects the programming of the season, so that all tastes, from the most controversial revival, are represented. It makes the maintenance of a high box-office level even more difficult, and budgeting becomes a job for a clairvoyant, but it never lets up on challenge and the maintenance of high standards for each production as it comes.

4. *Subsidized tickets.* All possible ways of bringing young people, the audience of the future, must be explored, but not entirely at the cost of the theatre. The view has been expressed elsewhere in this book that this is also the responsibility of others in the community, from whom assistance may reasonably be sought.

5. *Ticket agencies.* Most theatres outside London, excluding the big commercial touring theatre, are too small to farm out their tickets to agencies. Indeed, there are few such agencies which would be willing to make the block bookings which are a feature of the London theatre world. It can, however, sometimes be of value to both parties to set up a connection with a local shop, perhaps a travel agency or music-shop, because of the related interests and sharing of much the same clientele.

A caveat here. Beware of any such arrangement which carries the risk of the dreaded "double booking," which can create consternation for the management in a full house, and angry embarrassment for the patron which might well put him off attending a theatre again for months. There are ways of avoiding this, e.g.—

(*a*) Do not actually part with any tickets to the agency.

(*b*) Give them instead a book of ticket blanks of a distinctive colour immediately recognizable by the theatre staff.

(*c*) When the agency wants to make a booking a member of its staff should ring the theatre.

(*d*) The box-office manager should give the number and row of the tickets available, requiring confirmation by the agency then and there on the telephone that it is a firm booking, and double-checking the ticket and date details.

(*e*) The agency writes these details on the blank ticket. The box office marks them off on the ticket plan in a distinctive colour (traditionally green as in London theatres) and, *most important*, removes these tickets from the book to a special spike or box.

(*f*) The voucher issued by the agency then counts as a ticket and can be used as such by the patrons for the performance of their choice without more ado.

(g) The box office, at the end of each production, or at such intervals as may be decided, sends an account to the agency less an agreed discount, say 5 per cent. The details are made up by correlating the torn-out agency tickets and the marked seats on the box-office plan.

This operation can be a boon to would-be theatre patrons living away from the town where the theatre is situated and able thus to combine their theatre-ticket buying pain-lessly with their other shopping. There are hazards, of course, because of human frailty, both in the box-office and the agency, but the good-will and practical benefits can, on balance, be worth while.

FRONT-OF-HOUSE RIGHTS

These include the profits from catering and bars, and the sale of programmes and ancillary materials (books, magazines, etc.).

### 1. *Catering and Bars*

It is a fairly common delusion that profits in bars and catering cover a multitude of deficits. Would it were so! Bars and modest restaurants are amenities which add a great deal to the attrac-tions of any theatre, but they have to be carefully planned and most efficiently staffed if they are to pull their weight. It must be remembered that they operate for a very short time only. Though subject to the local licensing laws in respect of closing time, they are allowed to open only while the public are on the premises for a performance, unless special permission has been sought for a licensed restaurant to be opened independently. We should all like to have larger and more comfortable areas for bars and snacks, not only to increase revenue, if only marginally, but to enable the public to regard the theatre as a meeting place for leisure and not only for the two or three hours' traffic of the stage.

This function is served by the morning coffee which many theatres supply in the same bar used for drinks in the evening. Actors in rehearsal, the staff and the public are encouraged to meet over the coffee-cups, so that the public may develop a friendly interest in the place and its uses. The profit is small, the good-will valuable.

The better-equipped new theatres are also able nowadays to offer a snack or, better still, a proper meal before the performance, and sometimes even a post-performance supper. This is all very desirable but unless the theatre can afford a well-qualified and therefore highly paid catering manager, sufficient staff, and well-planned kitchen space, this is a hazardous enterprise. Catering can be let out as a concession to a catering firm which can absorb this comparatively limited organization into its larger and more profitable enterprises, giving the theatre a share of its profits by agreement. This lessens the risk but diminishes the theatre's stake in the planning of what is to be provided.

Theatre bars often present the appearance of a rugger scrum in the brief intervals, when everyone is clamouring to be served at once. With a staff and properly planned shelf- and serving-space however, satisfactory service is perfectly possible in spite of appearances to the contrary. No manager should be panicked into thinking that extra barmaids solve the problem. They will only get in each other's way, be queueing up to use the optics (the measuring devices on the bottles of spirits), and in general make confusion more confused. The guiding principle is to have a sufficient number of optics, cheerful as well as efficient staff, and a well-planned counter. Another aid to speed and comfort is the provision of shelves around the room, away from the bar, where empty glasses can be parked when the stampede back into the theatre begins. There is nothing more irritating than having to battle back to the counter, although many with little conscience push the empty glass behind a radiator or into a handy flower arrangement.

Cold shelves which keep drinks adequately cool and provide storage space in the bar at the same time are another useful amenity.

A pre-ordering system is another time-saving device, used with notable success at the Chichester Festival Theatre and the Yvonne Arnaud Theatre at Guildford, for instance. With this system, drinks ordered and paid for before the performance can be claimed in the interval on separately numbered trays— a useful service for those with forethought.

I say nothing of the old matinée tea-tray. To my mind the consumption of any food or drink in the auditorium itself is to be discouraged. The English mania for consuming ice-cream in theatres is not bad in itself, but the cleaning up of sticky cartons and melted ice-cream on the carpet, and sometimes on the seats themselves, is a revolting task. The solution is to provide sufficient space for all the kinds of food and drink which the audience seem to regard as part of the operation and to separate areas for the individual requirements, so that if one is only wanting coffee one does not have to compete with crowds of thirsty gin-drinkers; to furnish the theatre with easily visible receptacles for the refuse created; to have sufficient service everywhere; and to plan very carefully the access of bars, coffee-bars, etc., to the auditorium and foyer.

### 2. *Stock Control—Bars and Restaurants*

Assuming that the manager has chosen efficient and honest staff to be in charge of supplies, particularly of drinks, the stock control should present few problems. These commodities represent a lot of money and have to be meticulously accounted for. Constant checking is needed to ensure that there is no slackness and no margin for errors created by, for instance, a manager's sudden demand for supplies in the office, or his chance entertainment of a V.I.P. in the bar, or an emergency drawing of stock from the cellar for an unexpected demand.

The following hints may help—

(*a*) *Deliveries.* These should be checked on the spot, if possible by the barman against the delivery note. Modern methods of transport are not one hundred per cent reliable and a shortage of cases of bottles delivered by road or rail should be immediately spotted and reported. When there are bulk deliveries by breweries or wholesalers the empties should be sorted and put ready for collection at the next delivery. Bottles are not easily coped with in the cellar space, and may confuse the stocktaking or the advance ordering.

(*b*) *Demand and Supply.* The manager and barman together should be able to assess the popularity of various drinks or foods, and to cater for preferences. There is often a time-lag between the ordering of supplies and delivery, and this must be borne in mind. Allowance must also be made for seasonal demands and variations, e.g. iced lager may not be so popular in winter as in summer. The stock should be fairly wide in range to cater for the chance orders of some unusual drinks, but make sure the cellar space is not taken up by quantities of drinks rarely asked for. Make sure also that the stocks are used in strict rotation. This may involve manual labour in moving bottles around, but it is worth it. Watch the ice-cream too: do not let the delivery man go on piling new supplies on top of old in the refrigerator!

(c) *Display.* Plan your bar shelves so that the customers can see what is available. This again saves time wasted when people call for something they cannot see and then have to think again, often peevishly. A price-list should be clearly on display so that there are no arguments about prices when the drinks have been already poured out. Sandwiches and food should be displayed in a manner which also protects them from dust, cigarette ash and coughs and sneezes. Make this display as attractive as possible.

Be generous with containers of ice, water and soda-water so that customers can easily help themselves. This saves time and creates good will.

Make a point of cleanliness above all things—well-polished counters, sparkling glasses, ash-trays everywhere. Disposable plates are permissible and lessen the washing-up; china cups for coffee and tea are more attractive, of course, than plastic, but remember that they should not be clashed like cymbals if the washing-up goes on within hearing distance of the auditorium.

### 3. *Accounting*

All removals of stock from cellar to bars must be recorded and checked again with the totals of deliveries.

All sales of sandwiches and snacks must be recorded in detail after each performance, and a daily total rendered. The revenue must be checked against the bulk supply costs, so that the trend of profit or loss can be detected. There is one proviso here, to be remembered by the Administrator with nerves of steel. Sometimes it takes a little while for a new idea to catch on, e.g. supplying Danish open sandwiches instead of the more conventional ones, or opening a new counter for sweets. The Administrator must decide how long he can wait for an initial loss to turn into the breaking-even point, keeping a check on waste and loss the while.

Every counter and bar must have its own check-list of stocks and sales. Reasons for profit and loss must be sought, e.g. the shape of the room may be wrong, the counter too small, or the bar too far away from the auditorium. There is a whole history to be learnt from the figures and improvements can always be made through a study of them. Spot checks by the Administrator and by professional stock-takers should be instituted and maintained. Such checks highlight any slackness or inaccuracy, keep the staff on their toes and reassure the management that no malpractice is going on. The measures for spirits and the optics are also subject to outside checking to see that the regulations of the appropriate Weights and Measures legislation are being observed.

### 4. *Books, Periodicals, etc.*

Copies of the play, theatre magazines, revues, etc., all add to the playgoer's interest. The sale of these items can be regarded as an amenity with a variable margin of profit. As has been noted elsewhere, care must be taken by the manager that he makes the correct agreements with the trade organizations concerned, or he will offend local booksellers and newsagents and find his project forbidden. We should all like to follow the example of the T.N.P. in Paris and provide attractive, specially-produced editions of the play and other interesting literature, but this is not easy.

### *Inclusion in the Theatre's Estimates and Balance*

Detailed figures for the income and expenditure for front-of-house supplies should be shown under separate headings. Delivery notes, invoices, statements, and the detailed nightly returns from all sales, must all be entered and the vouchers retained for audit. Finally in the balance sheet it may be adequate to enter a total under Front-of-House Rights, say, but both for watching progress over the season and for filling in the annual financial statement absolutely accurate detail is essential.

Appendix III gives specimen forms which may be useful for some parts of this operation.

HIRING SYSTEMS

This is a very minor branch of activity but one which can be made self-balancing in income and expenditure. The hire of costumes on a large scale, as is done for instance by the Royal Shakespeare Theatre at Stratford, needs a separate department and staff if it is to be on a true business footing.

Smaller theatres provide this amenity on a modest scale to societies if they feel able to undertake the extra work for comparatively little reward. A permanent company which makes costumes to its designs for Elizabethan plays or others requiring elaborate costume builds up a modest stock which may as well be earning its keep. Amateurs can very rarely afford to make up elaborate sets of this kind and are most grateful for assistance with their budget through cheap hire of good costumes. Small hire fees need to be charged to meet the costs of keeping the costumes in good order, having them cleaned, buying hangers, chest of drawers, moth-proofer, etc., perhaps even of a small rent for a room to keep them in if the theatre building has no spare space.

Properties, furniture, recording of sound effects, etc., which have accumulated over a period can be hired out in the same way. Their usefulness for hire purposes is also an incentive to keeping them in proper order and easily accessible. Every theatre wages a constant war against the untidy accumulation of articles no longer in current use and all too easily pushed into a corner when a production ends.

It is helpful if lists can be compiled and circulated to organizations such as local amateur dramatic societies, schools who put on their own productions, Women's Institutes, youth clubs, etc. All these are keen on putting on plays and entertainments and all are usually short of money. If not a great money-spinner, a hiring system is a service to many sections of the local community.

EXTERNAL SUBSIDY

As far as national resources are concerned, The Arts Council is the backbone of State subsidy, and the manifold ways in which money is made available to the arts in Great Britain merit a chapter to themselves. Details are given in Chapter 2 of Part I.

Local subsidy may come from the Local Authority, the Local Education Authority, or from local industry.

### (i) *The Local Authority*

If the theatre belongs to or is directly controlled by the local authority, is, in other words, a civic theatre, its administration may well be part of the local government pattern. Its employees will be appointed by the authority and its finance will be finally the concern of the City Treasurer or the equivalent official.

Until the move for civic theatres gains momentum, the situation is more usually that of a subsidy granted by consent of the Council to a theatre company operating in the city, and incorporated, without any particular strings attached, into its general kitty. There is, however, whether explicit or not, a certain moral obligation to ensure that the money from this source does not just disappear into a bottomless well. Various ways are suggested in which it can be used for purposes directly beneficial to the rate-payers from whom it is finally derived. These may include—

(a) *The availability of the theatre to local amateurs.* Most regional theatres have weeks in the year which are allocated by custom to the local amateur and dramatic societies. This naturally deprives the resident professional company of the use of the theatre and thus involves extra expenditure of one kind or another. If the company is permanent, actors and staff have to be paid whether they are performing or not. It is possible for the company to go on tour. This, as is described in another chapter, is often part of the regular pattern nowadays. Touring is, though, an expensive operation and the standing charges for the building have to be met wherever the occupant may be.

The amateur societies cannot be expected to meet all the costs of a week in a fully equipped and expensive building, plus the hidden costs of laying off the resident company or sending them elsewhere to perform. The normal arrangement is to ask the amateurs for a rent which may or may not cover the bare running costs.

One way of ear-marking part of the local authority's money may be to use it to subsidize partially these weeks of amateur activity. Valuable and enjoyable as they may be for the amateurs, they can be disrupting to the professional company's plan of operation, and unprofitable too.

(*b*) *Special seasons.* There are very few companies which can operate lucratively at full pitch all the year round, and there is an increasing tendency to close theatres for a few weeks at some time during the year when the expectation of box-office receipts is lowest. This is often during the summer. At the same time, there are towns which, though they may lose their regular audience at these times, may have a floating population of visitors and tourists. There is sometimes rather bitter criticism that, though the local authority grant is made on an annual basis, touring and the period of closure reduce the number of playing weeks in the home base to a total far below a year's work.

A second way of meeting the local obligation might be to use the local authority's grant in part to reduce the closed period by mounting a special season for these slacker times of the year, perhaps with more popular plays and with less expensive actors than those engaged for the regular company.

## (ii) *The Local Education Authority*

It has been stressed elsewhere that the theatre is playing an increasingly important part in education both directly and indirectly. Money is sometimes channelled to the theatre for special projects connected with schoolchildren and young people. This again should not just go into the general melting pot but should be used and accounted for separately by some of the following projects—

(*a*) *The promotion of a special company for schools work.* Many regional theatres already have an offshoot company which visits schools, training colleges, and other educational establishments in the area with special programmes designed to promote interest in the theatre and, finally, to enlarge the audience.

The working schedule of the main theatre rarely allows time for the same actors to do this extra pioneer work as well as their regular performances. It is more practical to engage a special group of young actors and a lively young director who understand the children's interests. The gifts needed for this work are not always the same as for the more orthodox acting profession and the actors could not always be equally useful as members of the main company. All or part of the extra costs of this work, which include travel, publicity, possibly subsistence, etc., might reasonably be met from the special source.

(*b*) *Discussion days and study courses in the theatre.* Equally important is the introduction of young people to the day-to-day work of the theatre and to the complex processes which are co-ordinated to make a theatrical production. Many theatres now organize days spent in the theatre, for this purpose. The morning may involve the actors and directors in a rehearsal scene, the designer and wardrobe mistress explaining how the set and costumes are designed and made, a demonstration of lighting and sound effects, a mock-up of a stage-management technical rehearsal. The afternoon may be taken up with a Schools Matinée so that the children may see the sum of the parts which they have been shown in the morning. Finally, there may be a very fruitful session of open discussions afterwards between the audience and the theatre personnel. All this is very stimulating both to the children's immediate appreciation of what theatre involves and for the long-term establishment of an informed and perceptive audience, but it costs money—extra payments to staff and actors, even if token fees only, probably the preparation of slides, special recordings and tapes, etc.—for which external subsidy could reasonably be used.

(*c*) *Price concessions for young people.* Theatre prices are not so high in the provinces compared with West End prices, but even so they can be daunting for young people who have many other uses nowadays for their pocket-money. The theatre has to compete with cheap records, paperback books, cinema prices, etc.

A schools matinée can in its lowest terms be a way of adding a few pounds to the week's takings for comparatively little extra cost to the theatre, but the service of cheaper prices could go farther than this, often with more enduring results. There is no denying the value of an occasional mass visit to the theatre, but what we need to encourage is theatregoing by young people on their own initiative. There is an experiment afoot at the Royal Court Theatre, for instance, to make a certain number of seats available for school children and bona-fide students.

So far little has been done in the provinces to encourage this form of independent theatregoing and it needs developing. Schemes could be instituted to make the booking of tickets at reduced prices possible in schools through one of the senior children appointed as theatre representative. It could be made known that special tickets could be obtained at the box-office by children coming extra-murally, and some of the money from the education committee could offset the difference from the normal price and the loss of revenue to the theatre.

The operation of these schemes and of countless others can make the theatre's accounting more complex than the run-of-the-mill working. This should not deter any of us. Any variations in accounting schemes can be worked out to serve special purposes, and remember always that those who give money have every right, if they do not always exercise it, to know how the money is spent.

### (iii) *Local Industry*

More and more industries are becoming patrons of the arts in one way or another. This is not confined to the purchase of original paintings for the Boardroom or to providing canned music in the canteen but includes the recognition of the theatre as an amenity for executives and work-people alike. The executives may be relied upon to visit the theatre independently with their wives and families if it is made attractive for them. More co-operation is needed between the theatre and industry, however, via personnel officers, shop-stewards, etc., to make the mass of employees more aware of what the theatre can offer. There is no denying that the theatre faces a serious problem here. It has to compete with, and often loses to, the television, football, the dogs, the pools, etc.; but as they all advertise and sell themselves to the public, why does not the theatre make a comparable effort? Unless the effort is made, the light of the drama can remain permanently under a bushel for far too many people who have never been offered the chance to know what it is even about. There will never be a mad rush from the shop floor to the theatre but at least the nature of the theatre's work should be made known. Industry may help in various ways, some of which are similar to those used for schools and young people.

(*a*) *Organized visits to the theatre.* There are arrangements in some theatres enabling a firm to book and pay for a certain number of seats for all productions, to be distributed to their employees. A contribution from the firm may meet the gap between the special price and the normal one, a gap which over a period of successful productions with heavy box-office demand could diminish the theatre's income.

(*b*) *Special companies for factory visits.* The Royal Shakespeare's Theatre-Go-Round takes specially devised programmes of entertainment on to the factory floor, and companies elsewhere are following suit. It may be that these have no lasting effect, but anything which brings the theatre and other sections of the community together must be worth doing. At least for both parties a new window is opened, if only for a time, and this might well deserve some contribution from local firms to enable the theatre to meet their employees *in situ*.

(*c*) *Sponsorship of special productions.* The Board of a local firm or industry can hardly be asked to bestow largesse indiscriminately upon a theatre company. It might in some cases be more appealing to a prospective patron if he is asked for help with a special project. Such an appeal could be aligned with another facet of work peculiar to regional theatres—the promotion of local playwrights. The Belgrade Theatre, Coventry, has encouraged its local author David Turner, and the Victoria Theatre, Stoke-on-Trent, has Peter Terson. It is not beyond the bounds of possibility that a tie-up could be worked out between a theatre with this policy and an industrial concern which wants to become a patron of the arts and to strengthen its local ties.

(*d*) *Special commodities.* If actual cash is difficult to deflect from its normal purposes in the balance sheet of an industrial company, subsidy might well be in kind. Theatres have need of multifarious commodities. If these are donated or supplied at cost price, credit could be given for this form of subsidy. Very occasionally theatres might try out new processes, materials or equipment and serve the needs of both parties.

*Note:* None of these practices already existing or suggestions for others not yet widely used implies any obligation on local bodies to provide for the theatre's deficit (if they have one!), or any right of the theatre to demand such help. What they do imply is something much more fundamental—the recognition of the theatre as part of the community and the willingness on the part of the theatre itself to give all it can to all who can in any way benefit from the imaginative experience it has to offer. No theatre is an island, and its incorporation into the general network on which any happy and successful community is based gives it stature but also enriches all who are linked with it.

## 25

# *TRANSFERS FROM*
# *PROVINCIAL THEATRES TO*
# *THE WEST END*

A management transaction which was an unusual phenomenon ten years ago is now increasingly frequent—the acquisition by a West End management of a complete production from a provincial theatre for a West End run, sometimes for a limited season—a specific number of weeks—or of a new production of a play, perhaps re-staged. By agreement with the West End management the theatre responsible for the original production receives a percentage of the box-office receipts throughout the run scaled according to the West End success, with perhaps a lump sum for the physical assets of scenery, costumes, etc. This is not only a signal help to the repertory theatre of origin, and an enhancement of its reputation, but a contribution to the variety of plays which can be seen in London. The choice may be of a classic notably well cast and directed or of a new play which has had a first production as part of the theatre's declared policy with or without initial subsidy from an interested West End management. There is no hard and fast form of contract for such transfers, and the terms are usually a matter for skilful negotiation between the West End and the provincial theatre managements concerned. The arrangements may include a selection of the following—

(i) The outright purchase of the set, costumes and physical production assets by the West End manager.

(ii) Alternatively, the payment of a weekly sum for the hire of the physical production.

(iii) The payment of an agreed percentage of the weekly box-office receipts. This percentage may be scaled to rise by agreed amounts after the costs of the transfer have been recovered.

(iv) Possibly a share of the profits may be given to the theatre of origin, in which case the percentage payable weekly at the beginning may be lower.

In all cases, the management of the provincial theatre should make sure that all possible details are discussed and settled before the signature of the final contract. Their legal adviser should agree to the wording and implications of the final contract.

In general, the presentation of a production in the West End financed by a provincial theatre management subsidized by the Arts Council is not looked upon with favour by the Council. The subsidy is given for the work in the theatre's home area, and the hazards of the West End are too great and the sums of money involved too large for an Arts Council grant to be used for this extra-mural purpose. The permission of the Arts Council for such a transfer to a West End manager should be sought, with an assurance that none of the subsidized theatre's own money is involved. In addition, when such permission has been given, the Council has the right to ask for a percentage of the theatre's profits/income from the West End run, since the proportion of the grant used in mounting it initially counts as an investment.

# 26

## *TOURING ABROAD*

Tours in Europe and the United States are not restricted to the major national companies. There is a great demand for English productions of the classics and of modern plays and many of the established repertory companies are invited from time to time, often through the British Council. These tours are much appreciated by the actors, who view them as a kind of holiday, and although they are not undertaken for profit they are of benefit in that companies experience performances in conditions other than those with which they are familiar, see foreign countries from the angle of invited guests with hospitable treatment instead of being tourists, and exchange ideas with their colleagues abroad. Their reputation is also enhanced.

While all these possibilities are very attractive, there is a certain amount of preparation beforehand which has to be done very thoroughly to avoid pitfalls and problems abroad.

### MANAGEMENT PREPARATIONS

#### I. CONTRACTS
Companies touring abroad must be engaged on special Equity contracts, and arrangements must be made with Equity very early on in the proceedings. The sponsoring of any such project by the British Council of course makes the approval of Equity easier to obtain.

There are also some Continental agents, well-known to the British Council and recognized as reliable and responsible, who may undertake an independent touring arrangement.

When the approval of the trip has been obtained, it is usual for a sum equivalent to two weeks' salary for every member of the company to be deposited with Equity to guard against any unforeseen financial calamity. This deposit is of course returnable on the return of the company from the tour.

For companies receiving subsidy from the Arts Council special permission must be sought from the Council. The purpose of this is to assure the Council that there is no risk of the company's losing any of its subsidy on foreign touring, which is not included in the purpose of the subsidy from the Government.

## 2. FINANCIAL ARRANGEMENTS

### (i) *Main Contract*

It is assumed that the terms of the contract for the tour itself will be submitted for approval to all the necessary bodies concerned—Equity, the Theatre Board, the Arts Council, etc., after thorough preliminary vetting by the Administrator, the Theatre Director and the theatre accountant to make sure that all the details, travel, living costs, salaries, proportion of the production costs, lines, etc., have all been included on both the administrative and artistic sides. A margin of profit may or may not be allowable, but a reasonable figure for the contingencies which may very easily occur, under any of the headings, must be allowed.

### (ii) *Company Salaries*

(*a*) It is usual for payment of the salary money to be paid in bulk to the company manager for him to distribute to individuals. Before the tour begins, the management should ascertain either from the British Council, from the theatres where the company will be playing, or from the agent who has arranged the tour, whether there are any taxes which will be deducted in any country from the payments due to the artists. This ascertained, it is then advisable to work out beforehand in the appropriate currency: the rate of exchange likely to appertain during the company's visit, the salary for each individual with tax deduction, SET, graduated pensions, etc., as for any ordinary week in Britain. A bank official can usually be found to help with this, and an official list of salaries so compiled prevents any arguments with members of the company whose own arithmetic may differ slightly from the company manager's. This saves endless time and trouble, and any slight discrepancy can be adjusted either on the spot or in sterling on the company's return home.

(*b*) Some people may wish part of their salary to be paid into the bank for their families. This can be arranged with the foreign hosts through bank transfers, and is much safer and more efficient than allowing members of the company to run the risk of having to leave cash behind if the amount which can be taken out of some countries is restricted. Smuggling is not to be encouraged!

(*c*) *Cash in transit.* The company manager should have a certain amount of cash to cover the expenses which are so often not taken into account—tips for the conveying of the company's luggage across stations to catch trains, taxis to take the company to hotels when transport to and from stations abroad is either not included in the contract or fails to appear, telephone calls, even the purchase of medicaments for upset stomachs or sunburn. These may mount up to a considerable sum. In this connection, though it may seem an extravagance, if it can possibly be arranged it is advisable for the company manager to carry with him an emergency amount of money in traveller's cheques or negotiable currency to cover one night's lodging for the entire company. If there is a disaster or a missed connection *en route* this precaution can avert a dreary, starving night on a railway station and possibly a missed performance, or a very bad one as a result of exhaustion.

3. TRAVEL

### (i) *Passports*

Before the company leaves, the Administrator should find out as soon as possible whether visas and/or labour permits are required for any country. They are not always easy to obtain at the last minute. Passports should in any case be obtained from all those who are to travel, in time for them to be renewed if necessary.

The full particulars of all passports should be listed and several copies made. There should be copies in the office of the theatre and copies for the company manager to take with him. Such a list can often save a lot of time on the tour if it can be produced to customs officials, theatres, hotels, etc. It is of course absolutely invaluable in case of loss. The company manager may wish to keep all the passports together during the tour, but to my mind it is in general advisable for each individual to have his own. He may require it for cashing traveller's cheques for himself or if he runs into any difficulty while roaming foreign parts on his own. They can easily be collected together at points of arrival and departure where the company is located as a unit.

## (ii) *Tickets*

The Administrator should make sure that he has the tickets in his possession as long as possible before the company's departure, and the tickets must be carefully checked to make sure they are all there for the correct number of people. The itinerary must also be carefully checked and listed in several copies, both for reference in the office and for the company manager to take with him. As much information as possible should be obtained beforehand from the organizer or the travel agent about crossing cities from one station to another, the method of transport for this, the number of changes on the rail journey, etc., with times of arrival and departure at these points, not only for the final destination. Remember always that very much more time must be allowed for getting a group organized to leave a train, to find taxis or pile into a coach, or to straggle from one platform to another, than for one or two experienced travellers. The bookstall, the café, the souvenir shop are all potential traps and the company manager will invariably find progress slower than he hopes. When the company is split up among several hotels, so that the members have to make their own way to airport or station, it is often as well for him to give a departure time about twenty minutes earlier than the actual one, even if he has been careful to inform each individual how long such journeys should take!

The party usually travels on a collective ticket, and this is the safest way to guard against the trouble caused if any individual should mislay a separate ticket. Even so, all members of the party should be given clear information about the names of hotels, key people in the foreign reception committee, telephone numbers, etc., in case of missed trains. The company manager must also make sure that each person has always some money on him. If someone strays, the company manager's duty is to the main party, unless he can depute someone reliable and equally well-informed to look after them while he searches for the lost sheep.

If there is any variation in numbers, so that the total number of people travelling does not coincide at any point in the journey with the number stipulated on the ticket, he must inform the railway or airline officials. This may happen on the return journey if any members opt to stay on for a holiday. In addition, he should always check the times of flights or trains for departure as soon as possible after arrival, in case there are *ad hoc* alterations not known when the tickets were booked.

## (iii) *Luggage*

(*a*) *Personal baggage.* The weight allowable to the individual traveller by air must be carefully checked before departure, and must be clearly stated to all members of the company to avoid last-minute unpacking at the airport. It is useful also to stipulate that everyone must be able to carry his own baggage without relying on porters; this can be important if there is a rush for a connection, as well as saving considerable amounts of money.

Baggage will have to be collected together and dealt with in bulk in hotels, theatres, airports, etc. For easy identification, personal luggage should bear a company label, printed in distinctive colours and clear lettering, as well as the individual's own label.

The company must all be told about dutiable articles which must be declared. They must also be told that if they acquire in transit a quantity of extra belongings any excess weight must be paid for at their own expense, not the management's.

(*b*) *Company baggage.* It is usual for airlines to need advance information of the weight of skips, boxes, etc., containing properties and costumes, and, most important for stowage, of the dimensions. This applies also to any scenery, whether by air or sea. The management must make sure that this information is given as soon as possible, well before the day of departure. Coach travel also presents special problems in this repect. The storage space on coaches is designed for ordinary luggage, and it may be necessary for some seats to be removed if hampers have to travel inside the coach. It is as well to discover this before the coach is at the door and the company ready to depart!

For the Customs the contents must all be minutely listed. The Customs examination may take place before the company leaves and the baggage is then put into a sealed van. Lists must be kept in the office and the company manager and stage-management must carry a supply with them. The baggage must always be re-packed in the same way. In some foreign cities the examination is particularly strict and may even be conducted while the packing is taking place in the theatre after the last performance. Any addition or deletion needs to be noted and explained.

If the train crosses a frontier the baggage may have to be taken off the train for examination. The company or stage manager must make sure that the officials know that it must all be put on again and if the lists have been compiled efficiently the examination will be much easier. There is no greater ignominy for a company than arriving without its costumes or scenery because of a technical hitch at the frontier.

All the baggage should have the company's name painted on it as large and distinctive as possible.

### HOTELS

The management is usually informed about the number of single and double rooms available. It is best to work out the list of those willing or unwilling to share, in consultation with the company before departure. This saves a scrimmage when members of the company arrive travel-stained and exhausted and anxious to find their rooms as quickly as possible.

The company manager must check the financial arrangements with each hotel, making it quite clear whether the accommodation is to be paid for by the foreign organizer, the touring manager, or the individuals, according to the initial contract. Any difference of opinion or change in the agreed cost must be resolved at once, not when the company is on the point of departure.

Members of the company must be clearly informed about the payments for which they will be personally responsible, e.g. baths, wine, telephone calls, etc., and about how many meals are included in the management's arrangements.

### TECHNICAL TERMS

For the stage management it is a great help to compile a list of technical stage terms which may be needed in the countries to be visited if an interpreter is not always on hand. Even if he is, the knowledge of a few basic words creates more authority and confidence. There is a useful booklet, *An International Volcabulary of Theatre Terms in Eight Languages*, edited by Kenneth Rae and Richard Southern for the International Theatre Institute, and published by Max Reinhardt in 1959, but it is not easy to obtain. A little independent research will produce a good working list, however.

### PRELIMINARY VISIT

If the organizers can be induced to agree, a preliminary trip by stage staff and manager to the theatres abroad to be included in the tour can save a great deal of time and often money. Plans and working drawings, however detailed, do not always give the whole of the story, particularly for performances in open-air auditoria, where the ambience and approach are important. Photographs, details of the lighting installation, wing-space, dressing-rooms, etc.—all such information that can possibly be obtained in advance must be obtained as early as possible. Equally, details of the touring set, costumes, special effects needed, arrangements for borrowing properties or furniture on the spot, casual labour for pressing costumes, the construction of special pieces of scenery abroad, must all be gone into by the touring management.

In all, touring is a very exciting discipline for all concerned, and the final success depends largely on the thoroughness and forethought with which the preparations have been made.

# 27

# WEST END MANAGEMENTS

SOME fortunate West End Managers have an interest in the ownership of one or more theatres and the power-house of their operations may be sited in one of these theatres. In general, however, these managements operate from an office not in a theatre building. Their work is on the highest and most complex level. It involves the negotiation of agreements with theatres, both in the West End and for the towns which may precede or follow a West End run. The elaborate network of contracts with artists and members of the production staff, the commissioning and execution of the minutest details of the scenery and costumes, the rehearsal arrangements, publicity, etc., are all dealt with by an experienced staff. The legal aspects alone, ranging from relation with authors, artists, and all personnel to arrangements for performances in the United States and other countries, or the acquisition of current and forward rights in the production, require a detailed knowledge and a long experience of all branches of theatre. Managers conduct these negotiations, of course, in conjunction with experienced lawyers, but their own expertise is indispensable.

Administrative work in the West End set-up provides golden opportunities for bright young people with stamina who have worked enough in other branches of theatre to have acquired sufficient know-how and, above all, contacts. They have the excitement of being involved in projects with high stakes, dealing with stars, and top-flight designers and technicians. The manager's office work is comparable with that of a financier. Just as financiers rarely deal directly with the money involved, so the management staff are not involved in the day-to-day and domestic problems of a theatre building.

The House Manager's work is correspondingly more elaborate and complex than for a small theatre, though basically

the same principles apply. The Resident Stage Manager and
the Company Manager deal also with larger staffs, operating
according to strict union rules. A look at the NATKE agreements for stage-staff in the West End is sufficient to demonstrate
how far-flung his empire can be, and over what a diversity of
subjects he rules. The keeping and checking of time-sheets
alone for day-staff, performance staff, etc., almost qualifies for
a computer.

# 28

# THE MANAGEMENT OF A
# UNIVERSITY THEATRE

THE function of university theatre is a complex one, including service to the community by the provision of good public productions and the guidance of undergraduates towards an understanding of the theatre. The staff therefore require rather special qualities. It is not possible to generalize, since the relations of the theatre or department with its academic body vary so much from place to place, let alone its function within the public community of that area. *Vis-à-vis* the university, it is advisable that at least the Administrator should have a university background, which implies that he is familiar with the machinery of university administration. It is not always easy for the theatre to be fitted into a world that is more accustomed to dealing with the normal academic disciplines and procedures and is obviously more ready to acquiesce in demands for new laboratories than in the apparently more eccentric, or to some views frivolous, needs of a theatre. It is not in Britain alone that the needs and value of the performing arts have been slow in obtaining academic recognition. Even in so theatre-minded a country as Germany, the new and famous drama department of Berlin University had to battle for its present status with a full professorship.

The Administrator's university background is useful also for the understanding of the undergraduate attitude to drama, especially in universities which have as yet no drama department. Tact and firmness are needed to check the natural exuberance of students addicted to drama who hope to reach their goal by by-passing the necessary discipline and application. At the other end of the scale are those who, though doing it for pleasure, remain always aware of their responsibility to a paying public to achieve at least a certain standard of performance and presentation.

At the same time, it is essential that the Administrator's university background should have been integrated with a professional training. There are few university theatres which can afford, or indeed wish, to use their theatres exclusively as a studio-workshop for the department or the university. The box-office receipts are usually needed to augment the university subsidy, in whatever form that may be given. Professional companies frequently use these theatres. The Administrator must therefore be equipped with a knowledge of the professional procedure of negotiating contracts on the normal terms used in touring theatres and of the standard practice in publicity methods, box office and management generally, as well as of the techniques of presenting such productions. Only thus can professional companies be induced to visit theatres which are inadequate for professional needs, too small in box-office capacity and perhaps with too small a stage for a production to be put on without some modification. For the touring company there are compensations which are attractive, such as the presumably intelligent and responsible audience and the pleasure of using a new building with up-to-date equipment; but the audience and the authors have a right to expect that their productions will be presented with the expertise which they meet in professional touring theatres.

Anomalous though it may appear in a university setting, it is essential that the stage staff should be highly trained and efficient professionals. Just as technicians with a specialized training are needed for science laboratories. As a minimum, there should be a Technical Director, a Stage Manager and a Chief Electrician.

The Technical Director should be a man of quiet authority, experienced in the co-ordination and practical planning of productions, in fact the counterpart backstage of the Administrator front of house. For the student users of the theatre, he should be the source of general and correct theatre procedure, the forward planning and conduct of productions, and the practical adviser on technical matters, especially when no formal training is given. There is no other way for student users where there is no Drama Department to acquire such knowledge. He should be personally of the calibre to inspire the respect on which will depend the students' willingness to work under instruction.

Whether he is formally so-called or not, he must also be a teacher. He will also be called upon to use his knowledge and experience in their more usual channels in dealing with visiting professional companies.

The same requirements hold good for the staff under his jurisdiction. It is a truism in all management structures that the attitude of the man at the top will be reflected by his subordinates, and this is nowhere more true than in the present form of university theatre.

It is very likely that with the demise, whether temporary or not, of the old touring pattern, the new university theatre and arts centres now emerging will open up new vistas, not only for their resident student users but for professional theatre generally. University Theatre is becoming an important new area in its own right and in the general picture of theatre activity in this country.

## *Conclusion*

No categorization of theatre management can be totally satisfactory because the quality which fuses the parts into a satisfactory whole defies definition. Much of management technique is plain common sense, resulting in the efficient and pleasant working of the whole building and its staff.

A theatre is a microcosm which can absorb a wide variety of personalities and talents. School-leavers, for instance, are often amazed by the scope offered by the theatre world and by the fact that it needs gifts and training more generally available than those needed for acting only. It is expanding all the time and though streamlining may eventually change many of the methods outlined in this book it is difficult to see how the need for trained and enthusiastic people will ever diminish.

# Appendix 1

## *BOX OFFICE PRO-FORMAS*

---

### FINAL RETURN

*Production* ...........................................

*Performance* ...................................19......

| | | | |
|---|---|---|---|
| Doors | | | |
| Matured Booking | | | |
| GROSS Total £ | | | |
| *Less* Library Discount | | | |
| NET Total £ | | | |
| | | | |
| Advance (Carried Forward) £ | | | |

..............................

*Box Office Manager*

---

# BOX OFFICE NIGHTLY RETURN

Nightly Return...............Show.............................................Date...............

| Prices | Sold | Free | Open | £ | s. | d. | Libraries No. | £ | s. | d. | Disc. s. | d. |
|---|---|---|---|---|---|---|---|---|---|---|---|---|
| STALLS | | | | | | | | | | | | |
| 15/– | | | | | | | | | | | | |
| 11/– | | | | | | | | | | | | |
| 10/6 | | | | | | | | | | | | |
| 9/– | | | | | | | | | | | | |
| 8/– | | | | | | | | | | | | |
| 6/6 | | | | | | | | | | | | |
| 6/– | | | | | | | | | | | | |
| 5/6 | | | | | | | | | | | | |
| 5/– | | | | | | | | | | | | |
| 4/– | | | | | | | | | | | | |
| 3/6 | | | | | | | | | | | | |
| CIRCLE | | | | | | | | | | | | |
| 15/– | | | | | | | | | | | | |
| 11/– | | | | | | | | | | | | |
| 10/6 | | | | | | | | | | | | |
| 9/– | | | | | | | | | | | | |
| 8/– | | | | | | | | | | | | |
| 6/6 | | | | | | | | | | | | |
| 6/– | | | | | | | | | | | | |
| 5/6 | | | | | | | | | | | | |
| 5/– | | | | | | | | | | | | |
| 4/– | | | | | | | | | | | | |
| 3/6 | | | | | | | | | | | | |
| TOTALS | | | | | | | | | | | | |

Less Library Discount

Net Total

# BOX OFFICE
## WEEKLY SUMMARY

*Production* . . . . . . . . . . . . . . . . . . . . . . . . . . . . . . .

*Week ending* . . . . . . . . . . . . . . . . . . . . . . . . . 19 . . . .

|  |  | NET *(Library Discount deducted)* | | | GROSS | | |
|---|---|---|---|---|---|---|---|
| Monday | Mat. | | | | | | |
| ,, | Eve. | | | | | | |
| Tuesday | Mat. | | | | | | |
| ,, | Eve. | | | | | | |
| Wednesday | Mat. | | | | | | |
| ,, | Eve. | | | | | | |
| Thursday | Mat. | | | | | | |
| ,, | Eve. | | | | | | |
| Friday | Mat. | | | | | | |
| ,, | Eve. | | | | | | |
| Saturday | Mat. | | | | | | |
| ,, | Eve. | | | | | | |
| TOTAL . . £ | | | | | | | |

. . . . . . . . . . . . . . . . . . . . . . . . .

*Box Office Manager*

*Note:* This box is for percentage figures or other information which the management may wish to include.

# TICKETS

## Conditions of Sale
Either printed on back of ticket
or exhibited in Box Office.

---

The Theatre Management reserves the right to refuse admission.

This ticket is sold subject to the Theatre Management's right to make any alterations in the cast rendered necessary by any unavoidable cause.

Under no circumstances can this ticket be exchanged or money refunded.

The Theatre Management reserves the right to refuse to allow latecomers to take their seats until a convenient break.

---

*Compliment Slip*

---

(Name and Address of Theatre)

With compliments and thanks

Please check the tickets for date and price. Should there be any discrepancy notify the Box Office (address and telephone number) immediately.

In response to general request late-comers will not be admitted to the auditorium until the first interval.

---

## BOOKING FORM

PARAGON THEATRE (Address, etc.)

| Official use only | Date of perf. | Name of Production | Stalls | Circle | No. of seats | Price per seat £ | s. | d. | Total £ | s. | d. | Alternatives—please state date, seat position and/or price |
|---|---|---|---|---|---|---|---|---|---|---|---|---|
| | | | | | | | | | | | | |
| | | | | | | | | | | | | |
| | | | | | | | | | | | | |
| | | | | | | | | | | | | |

I enclose cheque limited to £.............. or postal order made payable to Paragon Theatre value.............. £

Applicants for tickets making payment by cheque and willing to accept alternative seats are requested to submit blank cheques limiting them to the maximum amount they wish to pay. The Box Office will enter the exact amount due.

Please return to the Paragon Theatre with a stamped addressed envelope. (Address, etc.)

Name ...............
(CAPITALS PLEASE)
Address ...............
...............
Tel............... Date...............

# PARAGON THEATRE
(Address)
Telephone No:

*In answer to your application I am reserving the following seats,*
*subject to your reply by* return of post.

| Date of perf. | Part of house | Seat number(s) | Price per seat | | | Total | | |
|---|---|---|---|---|---|---|---|---|
| | | | £ | s. | d. | £ | s. | d. |
| | | | | | | | | |
| | | | | | | | | |
| | | | | | | | | |
| | | | | | | | | |

I shall have pleasure in forwarding you the tickets on
receipt of your cheque or P.O. made payable to the
Paragon Theatre to the value of £    :    :

Please return this form with remittance, and stamped
addressed envelope to—

Paragon Theatre (Address)

To . . . . . . . . . . . . . . . . . . . . . . . . . . . . . . . . . . . . . . . . . . . . .
. . . . . . . . . . . . . . . . . . . . . . . . . . . . . . . . . . . . . . . . . . . . . . . .
. . . . . . . . . . . . . . . . . . . . . . . . . . . . . . . . . . . . . . . . . . . . . . . .
. . . . . . . . . . . . . . . . . . . . . . . . . . . Date . . . . . . . . . . . . .

## PARAGON THEATRE
### (Address)
### Telephone No:

## *From the Box Office Manager*

*It is very much regretted that the only seats available, at the time of writing, for the performance(s) you requested are as follows—*

| Date | Stalls (Price) | Circle (Price) |
|------|----------------|----------------|
|      |                |                |
|      |                |                |
|      |                |                |
|      |                |                |

*We are therefore returning your remittance value £      :      :*

*Please re-order immediately if you require any of the tickets specified above, with cheque and stamped addressed envelope.*

*To* .....................................................
.....................................................
.....................................................
*Date*.................... *Cheque/P.O. number*...........

## From the Box Office Manager

*It is very much regretted that, owing to the number of applications received, no more seats are available for the performance(s) you requested.*

*We are, therefore, returning your remittance value £       :       :*

*To* ..................................................
.......................................................
.......................................................
*Date* ..................... *Cheque/P.O. number* ................

PARAGON THEATRE

SCHOOLS MATINEE

Schools..........................................
Play.............................................
Performance Time.............Date...............
No. of seats........ Seats distributed:  Row...
.......No..................
                .............................
Cheque for..........received (Signature).......
                        Date..............

## Appendix 2

# *PRESS FORMS*

PARAGON THEATRE

PRESS INVITATION

The Editor

Dear Sir,

(Name of Production)
First Night          Day          Date          Time

    I have pleasure in sending two tickets
herewith for the first night of this production
in the hope that your critic will be able to
attend.
    If for any reason you are unable to use
them, I should be very grateful if you would
return them to us as soon as possible so that we
may know what tickets are available for the
public.

**FOLDER COVER**

(In distinctive colour and design
on thick card)


P R E S S   R E L E A S E
from
P A R A G O N   T H E A T R E
(Full Address)

Licensee or Manager's Name:
Management Telephone No:
Box Office Telephone No:

Issued by

........................Public Relations Officer
Press Officer

(whichever is appropriate)

# P A R A G O N   T H E A T R E

## LOAMSHIRE

Licensee                    Management Telephone No:

---

## P R E S S   R E L E A S E

---

Production: (CAPITAL LETTERS)
Presenting Management:
First Night:      Day:      Date:      Time:
Duration of run:      From            to
Directed by:
Sets designed by:
Costumes designed by:
Music:
Choreography:
Lighting:
STARRING:

Details, biographies, photographs in folder

# Appendix 3
## *CATERING FORMS*

**PARAGON THEATRE—CATERING**

Theatre.........................
Date ..........................

**BAR SALES**

...................Bar

Teas and Coffees sold over Bar

Chocolates sold over Bar

Total

Signed.....................
Barmaid

...........................................THEATRE
*Date*..........................
*Where sold*.......................................
**PROGRAMMES**

£   s.   d.

*Number Received* .......

,,   *Returned* .......

,,   *Sold* ....... @........

.......Teas.................@.....................
.......Ices .................@.....................
.......Squashes ..............@.....................
.......Chocolates ............@.....................
.......Songs.................@.....................
.......Selections ............@.....................
.......Books.................@.....................
...........................@.....................
...........................@.....................

£

Signed...........................................

# SALOON TAKINGS

Theatre.............................................

Bar................................................

Date...............................................

| TAKEN BY BARMAID | £ | s. | d. |
|---|---|---|---|
| Bar Takings....................... | ..... | .... | .... |
| Teas and Coffee sold over bar......... | ..... | .... | .... |
| Total | | | |

**SALES BY ATTENDANTS**

| | £ | s. | d. |
|---|---|---|---|
| .......Teas...............@...... | ..... | .... | .... |
| .......Coffees............@...... | ..... | .... | .... |
| .......Ices ...............@...... | ..... | .... | .... |
| .......Chocolates.........@...... | ..... | .... | .... |
| .......Squashes ..........@...... | ..... | .... | .... |
| .........................@...... | ..... | .... | .... |
| Total | | | |

**ATTENDANTS' TAKINGS:—**

Signed................................................ £

Barmaid.

# COMMISSION SHEET

Theatre............................................................

Wages and Commission W/E...........................................

Attendant..........................................................

| | | Attendant's Sales | | | Bar Sales | | | Progs. Sold |
|---|---|---|---|---|---|---|---|---|
| | | £ | s. | d. | £ | s. | d. | |
| SUNDAY | | | | | | | | |
| MONDAY | M | | | | | | | |
| „ | E | | | | | | | |
| TUESDAY | M | | | | | | | |
| „ | E | | | | | | | |
| WEDNESDAY | M | | | | | | | |
| „ | E | | | | | | | |
| THURSDAY | M | | | | | | | |
| „ | E | | | | | | | |
| FRIDAY | M | | | | | | | |
| „ | E | | | | | | | |
| SATURDAY | M | | | | | | | |
| „ | E | | | | | | | |
| TOTAL | | | | | | | | |
| LESS PROGS. | | | | | | | | |
| TOTAL (NET) | | | | | | | | |

Total Commission   .    .    .  £    :    :

Wages (........) perfs.  .    .    .  £    :    :

Total Pay .    .    .    .  £    :    :

    Less N.I.C..    .    .    .  £    :    :

    Less P.A.Y.E.    .    .  £    :    :

RECEIVED THE SUM OF   .  £    :    :

............................................................

## Appendix 4

# *REHEARSAL SCHEDULE*
# *AND STAFF TIME SHEET*

REHEARSAL SCHEDULE

COMPANY.....................WEEK ENDING..........

|  | STAGE | | | REHEARSAL ROOM | | |
|---|---|---|---|---|---|---|
|  | COMPANY | A.M. | P.M. | COMPANY | A.M. | P.M. |
| MON |  |  |  |  |  |  |
| TUES |  |  |  |  |  |  |
| WED |  |  |  |  |  |  |
| THURS |  |  |  |  |  |  |
| FRI |  |  |  |  |  |  |
| SAT |  |  |  |  |  |  |
| SUN |  |  |  |  |  |  |

## STAGE STAFF TIME SHEET

NAME.............................................

WEEK ENDING.......................................

|        | A.M. | P.M. | PERFS |
|--------|------|------|-------|
| FRI    |      |      |       |
| SAT    |      |      |       |
| SUN    |      |      |       |
| MON    |      |      |       |
| TUES   |      |      |       |
| WED    |      |      |       |
| THURS  |      |      |       |

Extra Loads and Get Out etc.

# VARIOUS FORMS

PARAGON THEATRE — STAFF CALLS
(for circulation to Visiting Companies)

Company————————————— Production—————

Wk. beginning————————— Sunday/Monday get-in———— Time————

| Department | Permanent staff | Number of additional staff required for | | |
| --- | --- | --- | --- | --- |
| | | Get in | Fit up | Performance |
| Stage | Carpenter | | | |
| Electrical | Board Operator | | | |
| Sound | Asst. Electrician | | | |
| Properties | | | | |
| Dressers | | | | |
| Wardrobe maint. | | | | |

Stage requirements:

Spot lines, clear
grid etc.

Available
6 black legs

3 black borders

1 black tabs

1 track

Forestage
Pit
Auditorium seating

The ground plan and elevation shows these variations of
the forestage lift

## DRESSING ROOMS

| | | | |
|---|---|---|---|
| 1st Floor – No. 1: 4 places | No. 2: 2 places | No. 3: 5 places |
| 2nd Floor – No. 4: 7 places | No. 5: 7 places | No. 6: 7 places |
| 3rd Floor – Large:wardrobe can be used by chorus if needed | | |
| Any remarks on other side | | |

THE PARAGON THEATRE

TIME SHEET

NAME . . . . . .

DEPT . . . . . .

WEEK ENDING

THURSDAY

196

FOR OFFICE USE ONLY

| | | | | |
|---|---|---|---|---|
| HOURS . . . . . RATE . . WAGE | | | | |
| HOURS . . . . . RATE . . WAGE | | | | |
| PERFORMANCES . . . . RATE . . WAGE | | | | |
| STRIKES . . . . RATE . . WAGE | | | | |
| LOADS . . . . . RATE . . WAGE | | | | |
| BONUS . . . . . RATE . . WAGE | | | | |
| GROSS PAY | | | | |

REMARKS

THEATRE

CHECKED
STAGE MANAGER

217

TIME SHEET

| DESCRIPTION OF WORK | | A.M. | P.M. | FLAT RATE | NIGHT & SUNDAY | STRIKES LOADS ETC. | PERFS. |
|---|---|---|---|---|---|---|---|
| | MON | | | | | | |
| | TUES | | | | | | |
| | WED | | | | | | |
| | THURS | | | | | | |
| | FRI | | | | | | |
| | SAT | | | | | | |
| | SUN | | | | | | |
| | TOTAL HOURS | | | | | | |

# PARAGON THEATRE
## STAGE CONTRA

Week ending_____ Company_____

### STAFF OVERTIME

| | Sun | Mon | Tues | Wed | Thurs | Fri | Sat | Total hrs @ 7/6 @ 15/- | £ | s. | d. |
|---|---|---|---|---|---|---|---|---|---|---|---|
| Technical Director | | | | | | | | | | | |
| Stage Manager | | | | | | | | | | | |
| Chief Electrician | | | | | | | | | | | |
| Assistant Electrician | | | | | | | | | | | |
| Strikes @ £1.0.0. each. | | | | | | | | | | | |

Total staff payments

### STAGE SUPPLIES

Total stage supplies

219

PARAGON THEATRE—ELECS. SPECIFICATIONS

for circulation to Visiting Companies

## LAMP STOCKS

2 × PATT 93
6 × PATT 263
2 × PATT 263
1 × PATT 264
6 × PATT 73
14 × PATT 23 BODIES
6 'N' LENS TUBES
10 STANDARD TUBES

12 × PATT 223
12 × PATT 243 (1 kW or
          2 kW)
3 × PAGS
2 × PATT 76 (A/A)
5 × PATT 123
12 × PATT 43

1 × 45 comp. 3 circ BATTEN
1 × 36 comp. 3 circ BATTEN
3 × 10 comp. 3 circ BATTEN
1 × 15 comp. 3 circ BATTEN
6 × PATT 49

---

'ACCESSORIES
2 × 18' BOOM POLES
2 × 16' BOOM POLES
22 BOOM ARMS
11 FLOOR STANDS-MEDIUM
5 BENCH STANDS
1 FLASH BOX
1 BOMB TANK
1 25 gall 3000 WATT DRY—ICE TANK
5 'STRAND' TYPE MUSIC STANDS WITH LIGHTS

---

ALL CABLE LAMPS ETC. TERMINATE IN 15 AMP BESA.
PLUGS × SOCKETS, HOWEVER 25 BESA TO STRAND
3—IN-LINE ARE STOCKED.

# PARAGON THEATRE
## B A R  C H A R T

### Stage details for circulation to Visiting Companies

| WINCH | | | | |
|---|---|---|---|---|
| 18 | | | | |
| H7 | | | | |
| 17 | | | | |
| 16 | | | | |
| H6 | | | | |
| H5 | | | | |
| 15 | | | | |
| 14 | | | | |
| H4 | | | | |
| 13 | | | | |
| 12 | | | | |
| 11 | | | | |
| 10 | | | | |
| H3 | | | | |
| 9 | | | | |
| 8 | | | | |
| H2 | | | | |
| 7 | | | | |
| H1 | | | | |
| 6 | | | | |
| 5 | | | | |
| 4 | | | | |
| WINCH | | | | |
| SPOT BAR | | | | |
| PROS | | | | |
| HOUSE TAB | | | | |

# Appendix 6

## *QUARTERLY RETURN*

PARAGON PLAYERS LIMITED

CASH ACCOUNT          WEEK ENDED....................

.................DEPT

| DETAIL | AMOUNT | TOTAL |
|---|---|---|
|  | £  s.  d. | £  s.  d. |
|  |  |  |
|  | TOTAL | £ |

## INCOME AND EXPENDITURE ACCOUNT

Budget Figures
for 1967/68
£

[related to the estimated Budget
under the same headings]

£                    £

Production Expenses
Salaries:    Management
             Company
             Stage staff
             N.I. & G.P.
Fees: Additional artists and directors

Stage Expenses:  Cost of scenery
                 Hire of scenery
                 Cost of costumes, wigs and
                            properties
                 Hire of costumes, wigs and
                            properties
                 Electrical hire and purchase
                 Authors' royalties
                 Artists' travelling and
                            subsistence expenses
                 Transport
                 Music
                 Miscellaneous:

Administration and Front of House Expenses
Salaries:    F.O.H.
             Administration
             N.I. & G.P.

Rent (incl. ground rent) or amortization
Rates and water
Insurance
Telephone
Heating and lighting
Repairs, renewals and decorations
Advertising and publicity (incl. printing)
Stationery (incl. printing) and Postage
Ticket printing
Theatre licences and Subscriptions
Travelling, subsistence and Entertaining
Audit fee (incl. accountancy fees)
Legal and professional charges
Miscellaneous office expenses
Depreciation
Closed period expenses (incl. holiday salaries)

£

£

£

APPROPRIATION ACCOUNT FOR THE PERIOD ENDED        19

Balance (deficit) brought forward
   (from previous year/or quarter)
Net deficit for quarter brought down
Balance (surplus) carried forward to
      following quarter

£

£

£

NAME OF COMPANY————————

———— FOR THE ONE QUARTER ENDED      19

Budget Figures
for 1967/68
    £                                                    £                £

Box-office receipts
Touring receipts
Receipts from Young People's Theatre activities
Receipts from catering sales
LESS: Catering purchases

Receipts from Bar trading
LESS: Bar purchases

Receipts from Programmes and Advertising
LESS: Programme costs

225

Cloakroom receipts     £

Hire of costumes, furniture etc.

Theatre lettings

Sundry receipts

Interest: bank and investment

Royalties received

Broadcasting and Television fees

Membership subscriptions (Club Theatres, etc.)

Balance: being net deficit for the quarter
carried down

£

APPROPRIATION ACCOUNT FOR THE PERIOD ENDED   19

Quarterly proportion of subsidies from: Local Authorities
Arts Council:
    Grant guarantee
    Commerce, industry,
    Television, etc.

£

Balance (surplus) brought forward
(from previous year/or quarter)
Balance (deficit) carried forward to following quarter

£

# INDEX

*(See also "Contents," page xiii, for main subjects)*